I0441922

Drain

The

Swamp

Dr. Robert Owens

© 2019 Robert R. Owens, PhD

ISBN- 9781075916328

All rights reserved solely by the author.
No part of this book may be reproduced
in any form without the permission of the
author.

Cover Art and Design

Dr. Robert Owens

Dedication

This book is dedicated to all the heroes who protect and preserve our freedom, to those who have given the full measure of devotion, to the wounded warriors, and to those patriots who have not lost hope.

Acknowledgement

I want to acknowledge Dr. Rosalie Owens. Without her encouragement and support this book would never have been written and without her dedication and expertise in editing this book would not be what it is.

Drain the Swamp

Contents

i

Drain the Swamp

iii

Drain the Swamp

Drain the Swamp

Drain the Swamp

Drain the Swamp

Drain the Swamp

Drain the Swamp

Introduction

The pre-programmed electorate combined with the usual fraud, imported voters, and all the dead people who never leave the voting rolls of the corrupt Democrat City fiefdoms marched in lockstep to the polls to hand America lock-stock-and-barrel to the Clinton Crime Family.

However the November Miracle happened and instead of the Sleazy Don following the totally corrupt Donna back into the White House the Donald won.

Enough people swallowed the red pill and were willing to at least take a shot at shaking things up before we're swept away by the unregulated immigration invasion and state sponsored outsourcing that low and behold we didn't end up with another perpetually re-elected hack.

Our country refused to follow the dictates of the elite controlled media. America refused to become the turf of the Sleazy Donna from Chappaqua whose word parsing motto should be the Bart Simpson anthem, "I didn't do it! Nobody saw me do it! You can't prove anything." We chose not to let the White House once again become Bill's love nest. We refused to let the George Soros puppet in heels move into the Oval Office with her rolodex of contributors both foreign and domestic.

So what do we have now? The Cartel and the politicians that follow them around like a children's pull toy on a string are screeching day and night the Russians! The Russians! They had Comey's BFF installed as the Special Counsel because of Comey's leaks. The stage was set for a sequel to the Progressives favorite thriller, "The Witch Hunt of Watergate."

What's a freedom loving constitutionalist to do? How about every time the Progressives issue a subpoena for one of the President's followers we issue one for a Debbie Wasserman Schultz, or her Pakistani IT money launderer, or Bill Clinton, or Loretta Lynch, or any of the shady characters who actually tried to fix the election. How about

Drain the Swamp

a Special Counsel to investigate all the scandals of the Obummer nightmare, Fast and Furious, Benghazi, Lois Lerner and the IRS, or the serial unmasking of American citizens for political purposes?

Why should we just roll over and take it? Why not take it and roll on instead? We won let's act like it!

In Drain the Swamp Dr. Owens uses current events from the first two years of Donald Trump's first term placed in Historical and Constitutional context to highlight the precarious nature of our Republic. He uses vivid examples and a laser focus to ask the question "If we don't stand up after the Miracle in November and demand that the swamp is drained when will it happen?"

When Crazy Bernie, Creepy Joe, Chelsea, AOC, or some other socialist gets elected?

You see, if we can't drain the swamp now the swamp is going to drain us right into the sewer of history.

Dispatch One

Fake News is Old News
In the Drive-By Media

You want some fake news? I've got some fake news for you right here.

"GOP Has No Plan To Replace Obamacare!"

That's the headline the Corporations Once Known as the Mainstream Media use to try and scare the low information voters. Nothing could be further from the truth.

As reported by Matt Vespa in Red State:[1] The GOP not only proposed alternatives to the monstrosity of Obamacare at the time they were advancing proposals even before BHO was elected. We can start with the five comprehensive health reform proposals introduced in Congress:

---

[1] *Red State*, 6-13-19
https://www.redstate.com/diary/mvespa/2013/09/0
9/republicans-have-introduced-alternatives-to-
obamacare-for-years/

1. Ten Steps to Transform Health Care in America Act (S. 1783) introduced by Senator Mike Enzi (R-WY) July 12, 2007.[2]

2. Every American Insured Health Act introduced by Senators Richard Burr (R-NC) and Bob Corker (R-TN) with co-sponsors Tom Coburn (R-OK), Mel Martinez (formerly R-FL) and Elizabeth Dole (formerly R-NC) on July 26, 2007.[3]

3. Senators Bob Bennett (R-UT) and Ron Wyden (D-OR) introduced the Healthy Americans Act on January 18, 2007 and re-introduced the same bill on February 5, 2009.[4]

4. Patient's Choice Act introduced by Senators Tom Coburn (R-OK) and

---

[2] U.S. Senator Mike Enzi (R-WY) 6-13-19 https://www.enzi.senate.gov/public/index.cfm/10-steps-to-transform-health-care?p=10StepstoTransformHealthCare
[3] Govtrack, 6-13-19, https://www.govtrack.us/congress/bills/110/s1886
[4] Govtrack, 6-13-19, https://www.govtrack.us/congress/bills/111/s391/text

Richard Burr (R-NC) and Rep. Paul Ryan (R-WI) and Devin Nunes (R-CA) on May 20, 2009.[5]

5. H.R. 2300, Empowering Patients First Act introduced July 30, 2009 by Rep. Tom Price (R-GA).[6]

In addition,[7] the GOP has developed a rich menu of potential replacement plans for Obamacare that are not of the centrally planned socialist sort but instead conservative market-oriented health policy:

- Individual Pay or Play proposed in 2005 by John Goodman; this is a minimalist version of a broader reform envisaged by Goodman built on

---

[5] Congress.gov, 6-13-19, https://www.congress.gov/bill/111th-congress/house-bill/2520
[6] Congress.gov, 6-13-19, https://www.congress.gov/bill/114th-congress/house-bill/2300
[7] *Red State*, 6-13-19, https://www.redstate.com/diary/mvespa/2013/09/09/republicans-have-introduced-alternatives-to-obamacare-for-years/

converting the tax exclusion into universal tax credits.[8]

- Health Status Insurance originally proposed by John Cochrane in 1995.[9]

- Universal Health Savings Accounts proposed by John Goodman and Peter Ferrara in 2012. This combines fixed tax credits with individual pay or play and health status insurance concepts along with Roth-style Health Savings Accounts.[10]

---

[8] U.S. Health Policy Gateway, 6-13-19, http://ushealthpolicygateway.com/vii-key-policy-issues-regulation-and-reform/p-health-reform/national-health-reform/models-for-health-reform/individual-pay-or-play/

[9] _____, 6-13-19, http://ushealthpolicygateway.com/vii-key-policy-Issues-regulation-and-reform/p-health reform/national-health-reform/models-for-health-reform/health-status-insurance/

[10] _____, 6-13-19, http://ushealthpolicygateway.com/vii-key-policy-issues-regulation-and-reform/p-health-reform/national-health-reform/models-for-health-reform/universal-health-savings-accounts/

- Fixed tax credits.[11] A variety of proposals have centered on using fix tax credits to replace the current inefficient and unfair tax exclusion for employer-provided health benefits. Two good explanations of how that would work are here:

- James C. Capretta and Robert E. Moffit, "How to Replace Obamacare," National Affairs, no. 11 (Spring 2012).[12]

- James C. Capretta. *Constructing an Alternative to Obamacare: Key Details for a Practical Replacement Program*. American Enterprise Institute, December 2012.[13]

---

[11] _____, 6-13-19, http://ushealthpolicygateway.com/vii-key-policy-issues-regulation-and-reform/p-health-reform/national-health-reform/models-for-health-reform/fixed-tax-credits/

[12] *National Affairs*, 6-13-19, https://www.nationalaffairs.com/publications/detail/how-to-replace-obamacare

[13] EPPC, 6-13-19, https://eppc.org/publications/constructing-an-alternative-to-obamacare-key-details-for-a-practical-replacement-program/

- Income-Related Tax Credits[14] proposed by Mark Pauly and John Hoff in *Responsible Tax Credits* (2002)[15] and endorsed by the American Medical Association. More recently, 8 scholars from Harvard, University of Chicago, and USC–Jay Bhattacharya, Amitabh Chandra, Michael Chernew, Dana Goldman, Anupam Jena, Darius Lakdawalla,Anup Malani and Tomas Philipson—released Best of Both Worlds: Uniting Universal Coverage and Personal Choice in Health Care (2013) which also is built around a model of individual health insurance subsidized with income-related tax credits.[16]

---

[14] U.S. Health Policy Gateway, 6-13-19, http://ushealthpolicygateway.com/vii-key-policy-Issues-regulation-and-reform/p-health-reform/national-health-reform/models-for-health-reform/income-related-tax-credits/
[15] PDF, 6-13-19, https://faculty.wharton.upenn.edu/wp-content/uploads/2014/10/plan-for-responsible.pdf
[16] 6-13-19, https://aei.org/wp-content/uploads/2013/08/-best-of-both-worlds-

- Flexible Benefits Tax Credit For Health Insurance by Lynn Etheredge in 2001.[17]

- Near-Universal Health Insurance Exchanges proposed in 2001 by Sara Singer, Alan Garber and Alain Enthoven (covers only non-elderly).[18]

- Universal Health Insurance Exchanges proposed in 2013 by former CBO director Douglas Holtz-Eakin and Avik Roy (covers Medicare and Medicaid in addition to privately insured).[19]

---

uniting-universal-coverage-and-personal-choice-in-health-care_081610171236.pdf
[17] *Health Affairs*, 6-13-19, https://www.healthaffairs.org/doi/full/10.1377/hlthaf f.W1.1
[18] U.S. Health Policy Gateway, 6-13-19, http://ushealthpolicygateway.com/vii-key-policy-issues-regulation-and-reform/p-health-reform/national-health-reform/models-for-health-reform/voluntary-health-insurance-exchanges/
[19] *Forbes*, 6-13-19, https://www.forbes.com/sites/theapothecary/2013/0 2/22/holtz-eakin-and-roy-the-critics-are-wrong-about-the-future-of-free-market-health-care-reform/#1a3db5ca6d96

Then there is the plan Bush the Younger actually proposed in 2007 which was shot down by the Democrat majority.[20]

It was a sweeping health reform plan that would have replaced the current tax exclusion for employer-provided coverage with standard tax deductions for all individuals and families. The Bush plan called for a tax deduction that would have applied to payroll taxes as well as income taxes. Moreover, if one were worried about non-filers, the subsidy could easily have instead been structured as a refundable tax credit in which case even those without any income taxes would have gotten an additional amount. This is the kind of policy detail that easily could have been negotiated had the Democrats been in a cooperative mood in 2007. They were not.

What's sad is that the Bush plan actually was superior to Obamacare when it comes to providing universal coverage. Remember, Obamacare actually does not provide

---

universal coverage. The latest figures from CBO say that when it is fully implemented in 2016, Obamacare will cut the number of uninsured by only 45%, covering 89% of the non-elderly. Even if illegal immigrants are excluded, this percentage rises to only 92%. In contrast, the Bush plan (without a mandate!) would have cut the number of uninsured by 65%.

And looking back even though that font of fake news "If you like your doctor," Obama says that he tried to get the Republicans to contribute to the creation of Obamacare however the record is very different. He didn't consult with them at all. Instead he rammed it through using legislative tricks and deceit.[21] It was an unconstitutional law[22] to begin with, and it hasn't improved with age. Even today Democrat leaders

---

[21] Gateway Pundit, 6-13-19, https://www.thegatewaypundit.com/2010/02/obama-tells-democrats-they-must-finish-the-job-ram-health-care-through-congress/
[22] *National Review*, 6-13-19, https://www.nationalreview.com/2013/10/obamacares-unconstitutional-origins-andrew-c-mccarthy/

continue to perpetrate the fake news that Obamacare was a bipartisan effort.[23]

So how does the soon to be extinguished and soon to be reversed and repudiated Obama regime react to the flurry of fake news in their allies the Drive-by Media? Why of course they seek to censor everyone else by passing the "Countering Disinformation And Propaganda Act" which of course is designed to stop anything that contradicts the establishment's fake news, disinformation, and propaganda.[24] How fake can you get?

And if his parting shots are not enough there is the promise from the Regulator-in-Chief that he isn't going anywhere.[25] He campaigned on Hope and Change and all we can do now is hope for change. Four years

---

[23] *Breitbart*, 6-13-19, https://www.breitbart.com/politics/2017/01/09/nanc y-pelosi-obamacare-was-bipartisan-legislation/
[24] *Zero Hedge*, 6-1`3-19, https://www.zerohedge.com/news/2016-12-24/obama-signs-countering-disinformation-and-propaganda-act-law
[25] Charisma Caucus, 6-13-19, https://www.charismanews.com/politics/opinion/619 70-president-obama-really-isn-t-going-anywhere-on-jan-20

Drain the Swamp

of anti-American foreign and domestic debacles that will prayerfully end as *We the People* make America great again.

Drain the Swamp

Dispatch Two

Science Fact Swallows Science Fiction

Not too long ago I began a science fiction novel, which has always been a dream of mine, and since I finally broke through the fiction wall last year with my book, *America's Trojan War* I thought it was time. I even had a plot that had been rattling around in my mind for years.

I began working in what I call Writing Mode, which is where I go when consumed with the writing of a new book. Typically I will rise at about four in the morning and write for twelve hours, sleep and repeat until done. Building on the years of pre-writing and research that precedes the first chapter I often stay in continuous Writing Mode for weeks at a time.

This process has led to the completion of a dozen published books and several more that are currently working their way through the publication pipeline. In my mind's eye I could see my long anticipated science fiction novel spring fully formed from my forehead much as Athena sprang from Jupiter's in the Greek Myth. The anticipation of a successful creative birth drove me on.

Here is the plot that inspired me. A couple of scientists who were also husband and wife, he a world renowned geneticist and she a programming superstar, decide to translate the human genome into computer code. Once they have completed this herculean task they decide to hack the code. When they do they are immediately confronted with the entity that wrote the code and transported into an endless array of parallel realities. In these multiple realities it seems each was the invention of another and like a reflection of a reflection in a mirror these wheels within wheels stretched infinitely off into life begetting life.

Through struggles, temptations, and conflict the pair of scientific Argonauts chased the golden fleece of knowledge searching for the prime cause. For they knew that every sequence has its beginning, and there must always be not only a first domino to fall but also someone to knock it over.

Then in what was meant to be a stunning and thought provoking climax our intrepid duo finally break through to the final reality and find themselves using their hacked DNA code to birth a new reality. Thus the circle is unbroken and life begets life begets life begets life in an eternal cycle and the prime mover remains veiled while the unnatural source of nature reverberates through reality.

That was the plan.

Unfortunately the reality of science fact swallowed my science fiction. First the CRISPR-Cas9 comes along.[26] This is a remarkable technology that enables geneticists and medical researchers to edit the genome by removing, adding, or altering sections of the DNA sequence.

---

[26] YG Topics, 6-13-19, https://www.yourgenome.org/facts/what-is-crispr-cas9

There goes the revolutionary idea of hacking the genome.

This was followed by a headline which provided the final nail in my science fictional coffin, "Lab-Made DNA Used to Breed a Life Form for the First Time."[27] This article continued to hammer away at my fictional ideas of creating life by introducing modified genetic codes into reality and thereby willing existence into reality. The author, Clyde Hughes, put it this way, "Lab-made DNA has been used to breed a life form for the first time by expanding the genetic code with the help of common E. coli microbes."

Not satisfied with dashing my dreams of wowing people with outlandish concepts the article added, "Scientists at the Scripps Research Institute in La Jolla, California modified common E. coli microbes to carry expanded genetic material which they believe will eventually allow them to program how the organisms operate and behave." As my imagination was corralled

---

[27] *Newsmax*, 6-13-19, https://www.newsmax.com/TheWire/lab-made-dna-breed-life-form/2017/01/25/id/770293/

by reality the following posts were driven into the now to confine my musings of the future:

"Scripps Research scientist Floyd Romesberg said his colleagues have created a single-celled organism that can hold on indefinitely to the natural DNA mix in synthetic-base material."

"You can think of these unnatural nucleobases as X and Y."

"Romesberg said the challenge with X and Y ... was that they would lose their code as they divided. Graduate student Yorke Zhang and Brian Lamb, an American Cancer Society postdoctoral fellow, used a tool called a nucleotide transporter to allow X and Y to be copied across the cell's membrane."

According to Zhang, "The transporter was used ... , but it made the semisynthetic organism very sick."

The author of the article interjected, "The researchers found a way to modify the transporter that alleviated the problem, making it easier for the organism to grow and divide while holding on to X and Y."

And finally the author and the scientists ganged up on me and delivered the death blow to my science fiction fantasy about creating life when they delivered this, "The researchers said their next step is to study how their new genetic code can be transcribed into RNA, the molecule in cells needed to translate DNA into proteins."

I figured why write a fictional novel about what is now reality. Therefore to compensate for this extreme case of Writus Interruptus and to live out the rituals and exigencies of my artistic Pon farr[28] I waded into the depths of writing mode birthing two new books which will soon be available. These books are: *Then Came Trump*, wherein I share insights about where we have come from, where we are now, and where the Donald promised to lead us. And *The More things Change the More They Stay the Same*, which deals with the development of the secular political religion

---

[28] Star Treck, 6-13-19,
https://www.startrek.com/database_article/pon-farr

which is jingoistic patriotism using the three presidential assassinations of the 19th century as case studies.

Reflecting further on the startling announcement that humanity now has the power to create life I am reminded of an old story.

A scientist says to God, "You're not so much I can create life right here in my laboratory."

God answers, "Is that so?"

"Yes, it is and I challenge you to a contest. Let's see who can create life faster and better, you or I" responded the scientist filled with pride over his great ability.

"All right," said God "let's give it a try."

With that God stoops down and picks up some dust and starts molding it in his hands and the scientist grabs his test tubes and starts pouring liquids back and forth. God pauses and looks at the scientist and says, "Hey, get your own dust."

Dispatch Three

Anti-Trump Demonstrations Prearranged Prepaid and Predictable

Just look at the hysterical reaction to President Trump's long anticipated executive order to limit the admission of refugees from seven countries.

How do leaders in Muslim countries see it? According to United Arab Emirates Foreign Minister Sheikh Abdullah bin Zayed, "The vast majority of Muslims and Muslim countries have not been affected by this ban. This is a temporary ban that will be reviewed within three months. It's important to take these points into account."[29]

For one thing except in the case of Syria, where a long civil war has made vetting all

---

[29] *Newsmax*, 6-13-19, https://www.newsmax.com/World/GlobalTalk/emirat es-ally-trump-order/2017/02/01/id/771397/

but impossible, this is a temporary ban of 120 days not a permanent or even an indefinite one. A 90-day ban has been imposed on travel here from Iraq, Syria, Iran, Libya, Sudan, Somalia and Yemen. Of the seven countries facing a 90-day ban, three are U.S.-designated state sponsors of terror, and the other four are war zones. This is about national security not religion.

If it was about religion why then were not most populous Muslim nations Indonesia, India, Pakistan and Egypt included?

These demonstrators, Schumer's tears, and all the hate filled rhetoric has been waiting in the wings for the first opportunity to show its ugly head. Our retired community organizer even chimed in with his two cents worth after gracefully keeping silent for a full eleven days. His unsolicited remarks doing all they could to delegitimize President Trump and incite the protestors at the same time.

How spontaneous are all these demonstrations? Make no mistake there are many people who just show up. Given the power of social media to motivate the couch potato revolutionaries to march in circles and hold signs someone else makes and supplies, it is no wonder anyone with funding and expertise can generate a flash mob. Who organizes and pays the organizers? That is the question. Since the media cartel is the opposition we cannot expect them to reveal who the puppet masters are. Luckily others have done the leg work and unearthed the evidence.

Several sources have not only discovered but published the proof that these protest provocateurs were recruited, trained and funded by among others George Soros. In an eye opening articles with titles such as, "Soros Caught Red-Handed Funding Anti-Trump Protests, Paying Protesters $15/hr" they not only tell us what they have found they show it to us actually showing the want ads used to hire the AstroTurf grassroots of the Left.[30]

While I heartily repeat and sincerely endorse the sentiment expressed in the

---

[30] The Last American Vagabond, 6-13-19, http://www.thelastamericanvagabond.com/top-news/breaking-soros-caught-red-handed-funding-anti-trump-protests-paying-protesters-15hr/

saying, "I disapprove of what you say, but I will defend to the death your right to say it." We must not mistake the ginned up outrage of people who are pawns of the limonene liberals with the heartfelt cry of true opposition.

If this was genuine opposition I believe the people would at least have their facts straight. Saying the President's action was a complete surprise when he said throughout his campaign he would do it is a first indication that this isn't well thought out. Saying it is a religious ban when even those who practice the religion it is supposedly banning say it isn't shows that it is disingenuous at best. Ignoring the fact that President Obama did essentially the same things when in 2011 he had the State Department stop processing Iraq refugee requests for six months shows that these protestors either do not know history or they are expressing the phony outrage of sore losers.[31]

---

[31] The Federalist, 6-13-19, https://thefederalist.com/2015/11/18/the-obama-

That mouthpiece of the Collectivist elites *Rolling Stone* provides proof that this entire reality show of protests was prearranged, prepaid, and predictable. Back on January 13th before Mr. Trump was even inaugurated, the discredited yellow-journalism sheet most recently noted for pushing fake news[32] rape accusations against innocent people in Virginia reported[33] that they had interviewed more than a dozen top leaders of the Trump resistance. The following is their outline of the conspirator's strategy:

Beyond direct action and street protest, five clear opposition strategies are emerging. First, leverage Trump's unpopularity and fragile governing coalition to defeat him outright. "He's going to overreach dramatically, and we have to be prepared to deal him a significant setback," says

---

administration-stopped-processing-iraq-refugee-requests-for-6-months-in-2011/
[32] *The New York Times*, 6-13-19, https://www.nytimes.com/2016/11/05/business/media/rolling-stone-rape-story-case-guilty.html
[33] *The Rolling Stone*, 6-13-19, https://www.rollingstone.com/politics/politics-features/meet-the-leaders-of-the-trump-resistance-124691/

Weaver. Second, where Trump cannot be stopped, constrain his ambition by bleeding his political capital – "raise the cost of Trump radicalism," says Frank Sharry a top immigrant-rights advocate. Third, blunt Trump's impact with political resistance in the blue states – and even the blue cities in red states – where Trump's agenda remains anathema. Fourth, get out of a defensive crouch: "The best defense is a good offense," says Sierra Club Director Michael Brune. Fifth, when in doubt, sue.[34]

So much for the spontaneous nature of these protests, as these facts are easily found with even a cursory search of the internet. Mr. Trump rode the crest of an actual grassroots movement. He found the parade and successfully marched in front of it all the way to the White House. Those of us who can remember what America used to be before the Kennedy Immigration Act[35] transformed the melting pot into a smelting

---

[34] Ibid.
[35] Numbers USA, 6-13-19, https://www.numbersusa.com/content/nusablog/bec kr/september-2-2009/ted-kennedys-immigration-legacy-and-why-did-he-do-it.html

pot[36] pulling us apart instead of welding us together want our country back. The elites who want to send our wealth overseas and import, support, and exploit enough voters for a permanent majority dedicated to collectivism will stop at nothing to derail our last best chance.

So buckle up and get ready for four years of escalating civil unrest with wall-to-wall coverage. People have complained about gridlock in Washington for years. What is coming is complete paralysis. The Left will attempt to make the country ungovernable. Their media arm, the Corporations Once Known as the Mainstream Media will do their best to make it appear as if they are the majority valiantly resisting the imposition of authoritarian and racist measures by an illegitimate minority government. This is what we are facing. Four years of battle.

Now is the time for all good men to come to the aid of their country. Yes, I know most

---

[36] NPR, 6-13-19,
https://www.npr.org/templates/story/story.php?storyId=5391395?storyId=5391395

of the Silent Majority are too busy working to spend much time in political activism. I also know that we face an army of people many on the government dole and many rich enough to finance a lifestyle of life in the trenches from their gated communities and country clubs. However, we cannot leave our leader out there alone to face the coming storm. We are all the support President Trump has. The Progressives have the media, academia, Hollywood, and the Democrat Party. Mr. Trump can't even count on the Republicans. Led by John McCain and Lindsey Graham these Never-Trumpers are reaching across the aisle to sabotage our re-boot of America.

Stand up! Speak up! Put those who wish to preserve the status quo and continue to manage the decline of America on notice that we are here and we will not rest until we make America great again!

Keep the faith. Keep the peace. We shall overcome.

Dispatch Four

They Want a Civil War
We Have a Prayer Meeting

The American Revolution changed the world. Our Declaration of Independence proclaims self-evident truths. That all men are created equal, they're endowed by their Creator with unalienable rights, among these are life, liberty and the pursuit of happiness. These words shook a world held in the vise-grip of hereditary privilege inspiring people around the globe. Our Constitution established a representative federal republic with a limited government of the people, by the people and for the people.

Over the space of 241 years we have watched as our constitutionally limited government grew until it's a leviathan running amok like Godzilla in Tokyo

smashing things and scaring boy scouts.
Today the Federal government is the largest
employer in America, states are the largest
employers in the states and counties are
among the largest employers in the
counties get the picture? Government is on
a rampage and unless Mothra is going to fly
in to save the day we have to deal with
Frankenstein-on-the-Potomac ourselves.

Such brazen power-plays as when the
Executive Branch under our now departed
and not lamented leader BHO issued the
Legislature an ultimatum, either pass Cap-
N-Trade[37] or we'll impose it administratively
through command-and-control[38] made the
dramatic changes in our political culture
shockingly apparent. Has our balance of
powers melted away under the glare of
executive orders, signing statements and

---

[37] CATO, 6-13-19, https://www.cato.org/blog/cap-n-
trade-ultimate-pork-fest
[38] *InfoWars*, 6-13-19,
https://www.infowars.com/epa-threatens-command-
and-control-economy-to-push-climate-change-
agenda/

ultimatums?[39]   Some people say this is
evolution. To others it's devolution. Our
hard-won and dearly-paid-for Republic has
been devolving into a command-and-control
all-encompassing central-state.

With political dynasties bequeathing
congressional seats like hereditary fiefdoms
it's becoming hard to explain why we left
the British Empire.

We have not only had taxation without
representation as congressional party-line
voters ignore their constituents we have
also had representation without taxation as
the perpetually re-elected Lords and Ladies
represent the illegal immigrants and the
professional welfare hammock-riders.

These big government social planners
believed they had achieved their community
organizing goals fulfilling a paraphrase of
Lincoln's famous quote, "It may be true that
you can't fool all the people all the time, but
you can fool enough of them to rule a large

---

[39] Reuers, 6-13-19,
https://www.reuters.com/article/us-obama-speech-
climate-idUSBRE91C09T20130213

country."[40] They believed the activist BHO administration would fundamentally change America[41] beyond the ability of *We the People* to even have a chance of righting the Ship of State.

However, if these would be commissars from the faculty lounge would have bothered to step 20 miles outside the Beltway obviously there was a counter-revolution brewing.[42] The Tea Party was overtaking the Republican Party in popularity.[43] It had already supplanted them at the grassroots of the conservative movement. By 2010 an avalanche of voters thronged the polling places demanding their country back. With a RINO like Romney

---

[40] BrainyQuote, 6-13-19, https://www.brainyquote.com/quotes/abraham_lincoln_110340
[41] YouTube, 6-13-19, https://www.youtube.com/watch?v=_cqN4NIEtOY&feature=player_embedded
[42] Thomas, Beware the Counter Revolution, American Thinker, 8-16-09, Accessed 6-13-19, https://www.americanthinker.com/articles/2009/08/beware_the_counterrevolution.html
[43] Stan, Collapse of the GOP? Tea Party Beats Grand Old Party in Poll, 5-25-11, accessed, 6-13-19, https://www.huffpost.com/entry/collapse-of-the-gop-tea-p_b_384618

heading the ticket in 2012, millions stayed home. However, in 2014 they resurged and once again gave BHO and his Progressives the shellacking they deserved.

Following the tactics of Saul Alinsky[44] brought the Obama-ACORN-SEIU coalition[45] control of the Democratic Party and the country but following the Cloward/Piven Strategy for overwhelming the system to impose an alternative system has to lead to a complete repudiation of this radical departure from traditional American politics and economics.[46] We aren't Venezuela . Even after decades of legislative efforts to progressively create a permanent underclass of government dependents who would follow their leaders to the next

---

[44] Discover the Networks, 6-13-19, https://www.discoverthenetworks.org/individuals/saul-alinsky/

[45] Malkin, The ACORN Obama Knows, 6-25-08, accessed 6-13-19, http://michellemalkin.com/2008/06/25/the-acorn-obama-knows/

[46] Straub, Is The Cloward-Piven Strategy Being Used To Destroy America?, The Federalist Papers, Accessed 6-13-19, https://thefederalistpapers.org/us/is-the-cloward-piven-strategy-being-used-to-destroy-america

looting of productive members of society the majority in this country still want freedom and opportunity not cradle-to-grave mediocrity.

We the People have staged a counter-revolution against this growing tyranny. Was it a violent revolution? Did we stage mass demonstrations, attack opponents, or try to silence debate? No, it was a peaceful, lawful revolution at the ballot box.

Remember the illegal and unprecedented assaults upon America that we endured from BHO and his regime. The imperial president used the EPA to impose the onerous restrictions of Cap-N-Trade after Congress rejected them stunting and strangling the economy with regulations. He used the Department of Homeland Security to change the enforcement of immigration policy and cook the books without any messy public debate by the representatives of the people.[47]

---

[47] *Western Free Press*, 6-15-19, https://westernfreepress.com/barack-obamas-deportation-scam-homeland-security-cooks-the-books/

Ruling by decree, "I have a pen and I have a phone," is hardly compatible with constitutionally-limited government.[48] We were told the administration had solutions. They shoved their prescription to heal the greatest health care system in the world with the big lie, "If you like your plan you can keep your plan. Period."[49] Like a pig-in-a-poke their San Francisco leader told us, "We have to pass the plan to find out what's in the plan."[50] They claimed to have a solution to save or create jobs while we lost jobs every month or created low paying part time jobs at best, a draconian solution for the man-made global warming hoax, a solution for endless wars for elusive peace. They said they had a solution for everything. It reminded me of the drug dealer saying, "If you've got a problem take a pill."

---

[48] CBS DC, 6-15-19, https://washington.cbslocal.com/2014/01/14/obama-on-executive-actions-ive-got-a-pen-and-ive-got-a-phone/
[49] YouTube, 6-15-19, https://www.youtube.com/watch?v=wfl55GgHr5E
[50] YouTube, 6-15-19, https://www.youtube.com/watch?v=hV-05TLiiLU

They said they wanted a contribution. Back in the good old change we could believe in days the dialogue of class warfare[51] repeated that no one making under 250,000, or was it 150,000, or was it ...anyway only the evil rich would have to pay a dime of new taxes. Many working people found out we were rich after BHO's first April 15th stand and deliver day.[52]

Everyone has known since at least that tax-cutting wild man JFK that cutting taxes increases revenue to the government and raising them lowers revenue.[53] Since the government knows raising taxes lowers revenue and since they said they were raising taxes to increase revenue what were they trying to do? Complicated tax codes

[51] *Daily News*, 6-15-19,
https://www.nydailynews.com/opinion/obama-search-enemy-president-beating-class-warfare-drum-article-1.368969
[52] YouTube, 6-15-19,
https://www.youtube.com/watch?v=7-SavgJlBLA
[53] YouTube, 6-15-19,
https://www.youtube.com/watch?v=aEdXrfIMdiU

are used as a way to incentivize and de-incentivize behavior.[54]

If you want more widgets give tax breaks for buying widgets. If you want less widgets tax widgets. Using that for a guide notice what was being pushed and what's being pulled? Under BHO we saw taxes on producers and tax breaks for non-producers, tax cuts for people who don't pay taxes and tax increases for those who do. Taking the money of producers to bailout the greedy, reward the cronies and support the lazy.

Executive orders and signing statements have been used in Republican and Democrat administrations for years to change the Constitution without changing the Constitution.[55] In BHO's USSA sweeping new powers by regulators threatened to make Congress irrelevant as an all-powerful

---

[54] Business Dictionary, 6-15-19, http://www.businessdictionary.com/definition/tax-incentive.html
[55] The American Presidency Project, 6-15-19, https://www.presidency.ucsb.edu/documents/presidential-documents-archive-guidebook/presidential-signing-statements-hoover-1929-obama

Drain the Swamp

Executive Branch grew like a malignant tumor.

We the People didn't lose heart. We didn't despair. In faith we knew it was going to be all right?

I remember how many of these articles I end during those dark days of the BHO regime with, "Keep the faith. Keep the peace. We shall Overcome."

Today as the defeated and rejected Progressives stage rallies, protests, and riots I urge the same counsel. The last thing we need in this crowded theater full of combustible emotions is either a match or someone shouting fire. The snowflakes and those who manipulate them combined with the fellow travelers and the useful idiots are like a bully pushing someone hoping to elicit a response. They appear to be hoping to spark a civil war.

I believe prayer got us here. And though the prearranged, prepaid, and predictable demonstrations and riots are meant to provoke us to respond don't let them worry you.

Drain the Swamp

Why worry when you can pray?

Drain the Swamp

Dispatch Five

Trump and the Deep State

Words have meaning. A word is a unit of language, consisting of one or more spoken sounds or their written representation that functions as a principal carrier of *meaning.* Rush Limbaugh is a master of the English language in my opinion on a par with Winston Churchill and is the undisputed American master of quips, labeling, and metaphors.

As if to prove the point, Rush has once again coined a phrase that sums up a cultural phenomenon. He has dubbed those Progressives embedded within the federal bureaucracy the Deep State. This label perfectly describes those protected by the civil service acts as well as those political appointees who might be termed BHO holdovers.

Drain the Swamp

The commentary flowing from the Attila the Hun Chair through the golden microphone recently shines a spotlight on the fact that the Praetorian Guard of the establishment are working overtime to overthrow the results of the recent election.

There is something reminiscent of Yogi Berra's famous "Déjà vu all over again" in all of this. It reminds me of the last president who was vocal about trying to drain the swamp. Richard Nixon set out to reform the alphabet soup of agencies that supposedly provide the government with intelligence. It turned into a game of who gets who first. The entire Watergate debacle was populated by ex-CIA[56] and ex-FBI[57] agents. The CIA reports were withheld[58] from everyone until the deed had been done, a president overthrown, and

---

[56] *The Washington Post*, 6-16-19, https://www.washingtonpost.com/politics/ex-spy-crafted-watergate-other-schemes/2012/05/31/gJQAh80uFV_story.html?noredirect=on&utm_term=.cb3d9bce292b
[57] Watergate Info, 6-16-19, https://watergate.info/burglary/burglars
[58] Fox News, 6-16-19, https://www.foxnews.com/politics/watergate-cia-withheld-data-on-double-agent

everyone involved safely out with the usual federal golden parachute of a plumb pension with a Cadillac package.

To catch lightening in a jar and see how this was all engineered and orchestrated see the seminal book *The Silent Coup* by Len Colodny and Robert Gettlin. This is the only book that tells the other side of the Watergate myth.

If you consume the bilge being belched out by the ABCCBSNBCCNNMSNBC Cartel you would think that our president was attempting to establish a rule by decree imperial presidency. That is what we have had for the last eight years. That is what he was elected to replace with a government that governs as opposed to rule. And that is what the Deep State is trying their best to avoid. A government of the people, by the people, and for the people is as about as far from what we have had as you can get. That is what we voted for. That is what our President is trying to deliver and that is what the preprogrammed, prepaid protestors with their fill-in-the-blank signs are trying to prevent.

However you call it; the Country Party versus the Government Party, the Perpetually Re-elected Versus the Flyover Country, or Them versus Us it all adds up to one thing a nation divided.

Leave it to Rush to coin a name for that twin headed bird of prey, the government party of power, the Fusion Party. These are two gangs of political hacks plundering the producers of this country bound together by their contempt for us and their greed.
They are bound and determined that they will not allow any motley collection of voters get between them and their swag.

Drain the Swamp

Dispatch Six

Trumpism and American Sovereignty

For decades the globalists have been leading us down the primrose path towards their fantasy of a new world order run by them and their fellow progressive central planners at the UN. Their four horseman of the American apocalypse; George the First, Billary, George the Second, and BHO never saw a multinational surrender of sovereignty they didn't like. From NAFTA to TPP from the WTO to the T-TIP they have sought every opportunity to enroll us as just one more state in their fever dream of a super state with them in control.

Currently the United States has free trade agreements in force with 20 countries. These are:[59]

- Australia

- Bahrain

- Canada

- Chile

- Colombia

- Costa Rica

- Dominican Republic

- El Salvador

- Guatemala

- Honduras

- Israel

- Jordan

- Korea

---

[59] Office of the United States Trade Representative, 6-16-19, https://ustr.gov/trade-agreements/free-trade-agreements

- Mexico

- Morocco

- Nicaragua

- Oman

- Panama

- Peru

- Singapore

The interesting thing about most of these agreements is that while we allow goods from these countries to enter our nation duty-free and compete with our own manufacturers our partners do not. They have various mechanisms to make sure our goods cannot compete in their markets. They add tariffs by any other name top our goods as the arrive and give subsidies to their goods as they leave.

This anything but level playing field that our leaders have subjected us to is economically the equivalent of playing Russian roulette with a semi-automatic pistol. It may be exciting but there isn't any way to win.

Drain the Swamp

Not only have we surrendered our ability to add tariffs to protect our markets against foreign disruption and the eventual destruction of our industrial base we have witnessed. It also deprives the federal government of a source of revenue which was once enough to run the whole affair without an income tax. It is not only these two negatives which point out the bad side of this bad deal. Our globalist leaders have also signed agreements that make American enterprises and individuals subject to the edicts of the bewildering array of organizations and boards which make up the strands designed to hold the American Gulliver down.

Finally in President Donald Trump we have a leader who wants to put America first! Finally we have a leader who is not dedicated to managing our decline but instead dedicated to our renewal. We have chosen a leader not to lead us gentle into that good night. Today we no longer must look at the sun setting upon us. Today we can see a new sun rise, a new morning in America. Instead of a leader who apologizes for our History we have a leader who proudly proclaims we will make America great again.

Case in Point:

According to the Financial Times, President Donald Trump's administration is preparing to ignore any rulings by the World Trade Organization that it sees as an affront to U.S. sovereignty.[60]

According to the Times the report says, "Ever since the United States won its independence, it has been a basic principle of our country that American citizens are subject only to laws and regulations made by the U.S. government — not rulings made by foreign governments or international bodies."[61] The report continued, "Accordingly, the Trump administration will aggressively defend American sovereignty over matters of trade policy."[62]

The Wall Street Journal also reviewed the document. They stated that the policy

---

[60] Reuters, 6-16-19,
https://www.reuters.com/article/us-usa-trump-wto-idUSKBN16832U
[61] Ibid.
[62] Ibid.

represents a dramatic departure from the Obama administration, which emphasized international economic rules and the authority of the WTO, a body that regulates trade and resolves disputes among its members.[63] The report also states that the Trump Administration will use, "all possible sources of leverage to encourage other countries to open up their markets."[64]

This is akin to a Second Declaration of Independence. No more will we continue to surrender our sovereignty, the sovereignty our ancestors, our brothers and our sisters have bled and died to establish and protect be diluted in the committees of nameless faceless bureaucrats where America has no more voice than El Salvador.

Strike up the band! Wave the flags. A campaign became a movement. A

---

[63] Talley,I. & Maudlin, Wall Street Journal, 2-28-17, accessed 6-16-19, https://www.wsj.com/articles/trump-administration-trade-policy-expected-to-seek-diminish-wto-authority-in-the-u-s-1488330361
[64] *Newsmax*, 6-16-19, https://www.newsmax.com/Finance/StreetTalk/Trump-WTO-Rulings-Financial-Times/2017/02/28/id/776170/

movement became a revolution. And this revolution is determined to make America great again!

Drain the Swamp

Dispatch Seven

Trump Protestors Professional Patsies

From the snowflake college students who
need a safe space to protect them from
anyone who might be cruel enough to
disagree with their progressive
programming to the America last crowd at
the DNC what we are witnessing is an
organized effort to over throw the
government of the United States one
protest, I mean demonstration, I mean riot
at a time.

In the New Speak of our Soros-funded
Alinsky-trained pink shirted fascists
diversity means everyone agrees with them.
Freedom of speech means no one says
anything they disagree with. And the
Constitution says whatever they need it to
say to do whatever they want.

How Orwellian can you get?

52

Drain the Swamp

Reality slips down the memory hole and those who railed against Trump for saying he might not accept the results of the election reject the results of the election. The ABCCBSNBCCNNMSNBCPBS Cartel pretends that all of this manufactured furry is spontaneous, the eruption of the grass roots. It is more like the reflection of a Jumbo Tron on AstroTurf. This isn't the people speaking truth to power this is the power using people as ventriloquist dummies to mouth slogans.

How many times do we have to listen to the Cartel broadcast their talking points, the same script from all locations only to find that low and behold by the next morning these very talking points are now the personal opinion of the sheeple who make up their mob? How many of our friends, relatives, and acquaintances profess loyalty to and cast voted for perpetually re-elected demagogues who support everything these people oppose and oppose everything they support? How many must we see to realize the dumbing down and indoctrination of our fellow citizens is working?

The newspaper nightly news late-night comedy show devotees follow their leaders and believe that the resistance to the Trump Presidency is organic. They even join the flash mobs and carry the mass made signs. I wonder how many realize that the planners and provocateurs who organize these protests have a training manual for protesting Trump?[65]

Paul Sperry of the New York Post reveals:

> Organizing for Action, a group founded by former President Barack Obama and featured prominently on his new post-presidency website, is distributing a training manual to anti-Trump activists that advises them to bully GOP lawmakers into backing off support for repealing ObamaCare, curbing immigration from high-risk Islamic nations and building a border wall.

---

[65] Sperry, Paul, *New York Post*, 2-18-17, Accessed 6-16-19, https://nypost.com/2017/02/18/obama-linked-activists-have-a-training-manual-for-protesting-trump/

Drain the Swamp

The tactics promoted in the training manual were used in the highly reported protests at the recent Republican Town Hall Meetings. Of course it was never mentioned that the Democrats were not holding any town hall meetings so that their followers would be available to harass Republicans.

The article by Sperry continues its revelations:

> The manual, published with OFA partner "Indivisible," advises protesters to go into halls quietly so as not to raise alarms, and "grab seats at the front of the room but do not all sit together." Rather, spread out in pairs to make it seem like the whole room opposes the Republican host's positions. "This will help reinforce the impression of broad consensus." It also urges them to ask "hostile" questions — while keeping "a firm hold on the mic" — and loudly boo the GOP politician if he isn't "giving you real answers."
>
> "Express your concern [to the event's hosts] they are giving a platform to

pro-Trump authoritarianism, racism, and corruption," it says.

The goal is to make Republicans, even from safe districts, second-guess their support for the Trump agenda, and to prime "the ground for the 2018 midterms when Democrats retake power."

"Even the safest [Republican] will be deeply alarmed by signs of organized opposition," the document states, "because these actions create the impression that they're not connected to their district and not listening to their constituents."

After the event, protesters are advised to feed video footage to local and national media.

"Unfavorable exchanges caught on video can be devastating" for Republican lawmakers, it says, when "shared through social media and picked up by local and national media." After protesters gave MSNBC, CNN and the networks footage of their dust-up with Chaffetz, for example, the outlets ran them continuously, forcing Chaffetz to issue statements defending himself.

The manual also advises protesters to flood "Trump-friendly" lawmakers' Hill offices with angry phone calls and emails demanding the resignation of top White House adviser Steve Bannon.

A script advises callers to complain: "I'm honestly scared that a known racist and anti-Semite will be working just feet from the Oval Office ... It is everyone's business if a man who promoted white supremacy is serving as an adviser to the president."

Does any of this sound familiar? Isn't this exactly what happened? The whole thing was choreographed and executed just as written in the training manual. Then it was reported as if it was spontaneous when any reporter who was even pretending to do his job could have discovered with one click of a mouse this was a put up job.

And the beat goes on:[66]

> OFA, which is run by ex-Obama
> officials and staffers, plans to stage
> 400 rallies across 42 states this year
> to attack Trump and Republicans over
> ObamaCare's repeal. OFA boasts
> more than 250 offices nationwide and
> more than 32,000 organizers, with
> another 25,000 actively under
> training. Since November, it's beefed
> up staff and fundraising, though as a
> "social welfare" nonprofit, it does not
> have to reveal its donors.

> These aren't typical Black Lives Matter
> or Occupy Wall Street marchers, but
> rather professionally trained
> organizers who go through a six-week
> training program similar to the
> training — steeped in Alinsky agitation
> tactics — Obama received in Chicago
> when he was a community organizer.

> Chicago socialist Saul Alinsky, known
> by the left as "the father of
> community organizing," taught

---

[66] Ibid.

radicals to "rub raw the sores of discontent" and create the conditions for a "revolution." He dedicated his book, "Rules for Radicals," to "Lucifer." Michelle Obama quoted from the book when she helped launch OFA in 2013.

Obama appears to be behind the anti-Trump protests. He praised recent demonstrations against Trump's travel ban. And last year, after Trump's upset victory, he personally rallied OFA troops to "protect" his legacy in a conference call. "Now is the time for some organizing," he said. "So don't mope" over the election results.

He promised OFA activists he would soon join them in the fray.

"Understand that I'm going to be constrained in what I do with all of you until I am again a private citizen, but that's not so far off," he said. "You're going to see me early next year, and we're going to be in a position where we can start cooking up all kinds of great stuff."

Added the ex-president: "I promise you that next year Michelle and I are going to be right there with you, and the clouds are going to start parting, and we're going to be busy. I've got all kinds of thoughts and ideas about it, but this isn't the best time to share them. Point is, I'm still fired up and ready to go, and I hope that all of you are, as well."

The New York Post among other news organizations is doing the leg work. The information is readily available for anyone who is interested. These poor dupes who are out there screaming and marching have been pre-programmed by years of government education and decades of televised propaganda. They honestly believe whatever the Cartel says is their personal opinion. They aren't evil they are merely following and supporting evil. Lenin called them useful idiots. That seems a bit harsh so maybe we could give them the benefit of the doubt and just call them professional patsies?

Drain the Swamp

Dispatch Eight

President Trump Follow Your Own Advice

Numerous times the President has said in his opinion the Republicans should let Obamacare alone for a year or two. Let it implode (as it was designed to do) while the Democrats still own it.

When President Trump gave his well-received speech at CPAC he said that he has told Speaker of the House Paul Ryan and the Republican leadership in Congress to simply "let it implode." The law is simply "repealing itself," Trump told the audience. "All we have to do is let it implode."[67] He tweeted Jan. 4, "Republicans must be careful in that the Dems own the failed

---

[67] Donache, Robert, *The Daily Caller*, 2-24-17, accessed 6-16-19, https://dailycaller.com/2017/02/24/trump-i-tell-rep-leadership-let-obamacare-implode/

61

ObamaCare disaster, with its poor coverage and massive premium increases......"[68]

On another occasion the President said to Health and Human Services Secretary Tom Price, "I've been telling you why don't we wait, just let it implode and let's not take the blame." After a recent listening session with the GOP in Congress the President elaborated further:

> And I have to say this, just in closing, and then I want to hear some of your stories. And we'll let the press stay for your stories, if you like, but the press is making Obamacare look so good all of a sudden. I'm watching the news. It looks so good. They're showing these reports — now, this one gets so much and this one gets so much.
>
> First of all, it covers very few people. And it's imploding. And '17 will be the worst year. And I said it once, I'll say it again. Because Obama's gone — you know, he — things are going to be very bad this

---

[68] Twitter, https://twitter.com/realDonaldTrump/status/816644 321768312832

year for the people with Obamacare.
They're gonna have tremendous
increases. And the Republicans, frankly,
are putting themselves in a very bad
position — I tell this to Tom Price all the
time — by repealing Obamacare.
Because people aren't going to see the
truly devastating effects of Obamacare.
They're not gonna see the devastation in
'17 and '18 and '19. It'll be gone by then.
It'll — whether we do it or not, it'll be
imploded off the map.

So, the press is making it look so
wonderful so that if we end it, everyone's
going to say, "Oh, remember how great
Obamacare used to be? Remember how
wonderful it used to be? It was so great.

It's a little bit like President Obama.
When he left, people liked him. When he
was here, people didn't like him so much.
That's the way life goes. That's human
nature.

The fact is, Obamacare is a disaster. And
by — and I say this to the Republicans all
the time — by repealing it, by getting rid
of it, by ending it, everyone's gonna say,

"Oh, it used to be so great." But it wasn't great.

And I tell Tom Price and I tell Paul Ryan, I tell everyone of 'em, I say the best thing you can do politically is wait a year because it's gonna blow itself off the map. But that's the wrong thing to do for the country. It's the wrong thing to do for our citizens.

Mr. President follow your own advice. Let this monstrosity implode and let the Democrats who shoved it down our throats take the blame. Don't sign on to Speaker Ryan's halfhearted attempt to shove Obamacare Lite down our throats as a remedy. If you fall into this trap you may well be sinking your presidency. The ABCCBSNBCCNNMASNBCPBS Cartel will hang this around your neck. They will drag out example after example of people who have lost insurance and/or died because you repealed what was meant to be a failure in the first place.

The Democrats passed Obamacare knowing it would implode so that Hillary could then say, "See halfway measures won't work.

We need a one payer system." That was the plan all along as pointed out repeatedly in this column and by many other observers. However you, this movement, and your upset victory became the fly in their snake oil ointment. Don't let them snatch victory from the jaws of defeat by getting them off the hook while impaling yourself.

There is Medicaid for the truly indigent and SSI for millions who cannot help themselves. We have a social safety net that is not enmeshed in the Obamacare nightmare. Drop this grenade. Dodge this bullet. Give us tax reform. Give us regulatory reform. Let the Democrats and their Obamacare die by a thousand cuts, and instead of rescuing them, make America great again by making America free again.

Drain the Swamp

Dispatch Nine

Trump the Chumps

This is it. This is the last chance we have of returning our nation to an agenda of America First. If the globalists among the perpetually re-elected twin headed bird of prey that is the best Congress money can buy along with their Deep State/Permanent Government allies can successfully thwart this attempt to make America Great Again there will be no reprieve. The stenographers of the Democrat Party, the ABCCBSNBCCNNMSNBCPBS Cartel media megaphone trumpets their fake news every day. Within hours this becomes the personal opinion of their legions of militantly apathetic low information voters.

The last person elected president who wanted to drain the swamp was Nixon in 1972. Before that it was JFK. Mr. President, watch your back. The RINOs in

Drain the Swamp

Congress along with their brethren across the aisle are planning the Nixon treatment for you. Let us pray there is no one planning the JFK treatment.

America has been sold down the river for so long many people have come to enjoy the ride. Like paying customers on an amusement ride they float along through the tunnel of entitlements not knowing that at the end of the tunnel is a waterfall called austerity. You just simply cannot continue to spend more than you make forever. While it may sound like fun to charge your overdrawn Mastercard to your Visa and your overdrawn Visa to your Discover and then get a cash advance on your Mastercard to pay your Discover eventually you run out of other people's money

We have been following the pipers on our way to bankruptcy like rats out of Hamelin. The music sounded great, "♪ You can have it all for free ♫" but eventually you have to pay the piper.

President Trump's first budget is a down payment on a debt too big to be paid. It is a stretch to believe we could ever see twenty trillion dollars paid off in our lifetime but we can make a start. We can begin to scratch our way out of the hole our out of control spending has dug.

Have you ever heard of the scratch test? An old man, the descendant of a band of robbers from Italy once told me that in the Old Country they would throw new born babies into a marble pool and if the baby did not at least scratch at the side in an attempt to live they would let it drown.

Another old story is that if you find yourself stuck in a hole the first thing to do is stop digging.

Support the President's Budget. Ignore the Cartel and their fake news. Let you senators and congress person know you want them to support the president. In other words, "Trump the chumps, stay the course and make America great again."

Drain the Swamp

Dispatch Ten

I Care More Than You Care See My Ribbon

For over twenty years my wife and I were the pastors of churches and leaders of ministries. Everywhere we ministered we founded programs to feed and clothe those who needed assistance. These ministries through the work of volunteers and the donations of private citizens fed and clothed thousands all without ever taking a dime of government money.

Back in the dream time when I was young in the ministry I helped start a feeding ministry. We fed so many needy people with groceries and had so many coming for hot meals it was astounding. We did no means testing. We fed everyone who came to the door all with volunteers and private donations.

Then came the Reagan food giveaway program and everything changed.[69] If you don't remember this it was a program started in 1983 by the Reagan administration. They opened the government warehouses and began giving away vast amounts of the American processed cheese, cheddar cheese, corn meal, non-fat dry milk and honey that was stored as part of the agricultural policy of buying up products to maintain prices. In the past this food was allowed to sit in these warehouses until it rotted and was thrown away. So instead of this wasteful procedure President Reagan wanted the food given to the needy.

When our feeding program was contacted by some state officials they said come and get all you want no strings attached. So we did. And we watched as our program grew and grew. The Federal Government of Ronald Reagan said no strings however in the spirit of his New Federalism he gave the

---

[69] Hillgrin, S., UPI, 8-2-83, Accessed 6-16-19, https://www.upi.com/Archives/1983/08/02/The-Reagan-administration-will-give-more-government-owned-food-to/7248428644800/

food to the States to distribute to agencies and thus to the needy[70]. This worked great......for a while.

Then the State wanted an accounting of how much we gave and to how many. That was fine. It was none intrusive so we compiled that and submitted it to the State. Then they wanted to know where the recipients of the food lived. That was fine. It was none intrusive so we compiled that and submitted it to the State. Then they wanted to know how much money the made and had. Then we quit the program. With this my first experience with founding and running a ministry to help others I learned a powerful lesson. Once the government camel gets its nose in the tent it wants to inch-by-inch take over. I vowed never again.

Every program to help the needy my wife and I ever started never means tested anyone. We never reported anything to anyone and we didn't have to because

---

[70] CQ Researcher, 6-16-19, http://library.cqpress.com/cqresearcher/document.php?id=cqresrre1981040300

everything was done by the churches and ministries we served and supported by volunteers and private donations. Many times we were asked about not means testing. People would ask, "Don't you know some people are gaming the system?" We would answer, "Yes we're sure there are some gaming the system but those who really need the help don't need to be subjected to embarrassing questions. Let's preserve their dignity while we help them keep body and soul together. If some are taking what they don't really need and thus depriving others with real need that is on them."

Why am I relating this bit of personal history? Not because I need a pat on the back. I have received more than enough recognition for merely doing what I felt the Lord showed me to do with the help and support of others. Pastors always get more than enough gratitude for things many are involved in. No, I'm sharing this to highlight the fact that much good can be done without government support and that the strings government support always drag along behind cause distortions, maladjustments, and inequalities in the services provided.

Why do I think such a lesson is needed at this time? The recent release of the President Trump's first budget proposal signaled the desire of our Mr. Trump to return the Federal Government to its original purposes, national defense, international trade, and foreign relations. To do this many sacred cows were brought to the block. Some of the cuts such as the National Endowment for the Arts, the National Endowment for the Humanities, and the Corporation for Public Broadcasting aim to shut down what are obviously Progressive jobs programs part and parcel of the social engineering and propaganda arm of the Democrat Party.[71]

However proposed cuts to other programs such as Meals on Wheels and Head Start are

---

[71] Naylor, Brian, NPR, 3-16-17, accessed 6-16-19, https://www.npr.org/2017/03/16/520401246/trumps-budget-plan-cuts-funding-for-arts-humanities-and-public-media

characterized as examples of the hard hearts of anyone who isn't a Progressive.[72]

This is what I want to draw attention to. This is the idea that it is the job of the Federal Government to feed and clothe its citizens. This is based on the idea that government can be compassionate. Progressives from both the Democrat and the Republican side of the government party say this is what's needed for compassion's sake when in reality it is what is needed for the sake of power. A Government is incapable of being compassionate. Compassion is a human emotion and a government is a bureaucratic organization that rules over a territory and a population. So-called government compassion merely establishes programs that choose who to help, who to ignore, and who to enrich. Mainly it is the bureaucrats administering the program and their favorite voting blocks.

---

[72] Levitz, Eric, *Intelligencer*, 3-16-17, accessed 6-16-19, http://nymag.com/intelligencer/2017/03/white-house-says-cutting-meals-on-wheels-is-compassionate.html?gtm=bottom

Drain the Swamp

A government cannot show compassion by giving of its own to help another. A government cannot expend one dollar on anyone that it has not appropriated from someone else. And once it has appropriated that dollar it siphons off a large percentage to cover administrative costs. It also requires paper work at every level as do all bureaucracies. Therefore instead of the compassion of you or me giving our own dollar to help someone, all of which goes to the other person government takes a dollar from someone and then gives a fraction of that dollar to someone else after making that person jump through hoops to get it.

That isn't compassion. That is governmental over reach. Progressives love the government approach. That way they don't have to give anything personally and they don't have to associate with those actually in need. Instead they can tax everyone else to pay for their personal hobby horse causes and then hire professional do gooders to do the distribution, all nice neat and out of the way.

All this taxation for governmental faux compassion drains away funds from individuals and private organizations who work selflessly to meet the needs of others. It also engenders a feeling among those taxed to pay for the Progressives pet programs that they gave at the office thus cutting into possible donations to private groups. This round robin effect of governmental interference in the instinctive compassion of the American people erodes the character of our people and curtails the amount of resources actually available for those in need.

Instead of the genuine satisfaction one feels from living out the reality that giving is better than receiving Americans are conditioned to think if they pay their taxes and wear the appropriate color ribbon they have done their duty to help make the world a better place.

The commands of government are enforced through the power of the state. The state can take your money and do what they think is best. The perpetually re-elected tell us constantly that they will bring the bacon home. When I ran for public office my favorite thing to tell voters was that, "I'm not running to bring the bacon home I'm running to leave the hog with the farmer that raised it." This was and is my belief of how it should be it was not however what you could call a winning slogan.

Looking again at commands we all know we must follow the commands of the government since they have an exclusive right to the use of force and they have shown over and over they are not slow to use it. However, as far as me and my house we will follow the Lord and he has given us the two most important commands of all, "You shall love the Lord your God with all your heart, with all your soul, and with all your mind. This is the first and great commandment. And the second is like it: You shall love your neighbor as yourself."

To my mind and my spirit that says it all. If we love our neighbor as we love ourselves we will show all the compassion needed and we won't need any bureaucrat to command us to do so.

Drain the Swamp

Dispatch Eleven

Is Anyone Watching Those Who Watch Us?

The ongoing tempest in a tea cup concerning Russian hacking and Trump collusion is merely "Why? Oh, why did Hillary lose?" etched out in Washington double speak through the media megaphone. To sum it all up I'm reminded of a quote from the Wicked Witch of the West, "What a world...what a world." (Not THAT Wicked Witch of the West the one from the Wizard of Oz.)

Here we are in an America where the government can listen to and record every word or keystroke without a warrant and the person who tells us about it is a traitor. This is an America obsessed with a manufactured scandal about Russian collusion to elect Trump by people who love to say, "Hillary won the popular vote." They never seem to connect the dots. If the

Drain the Swamp

Russians hacked our election and Hillary won the popular vote whose side were they on?

Back in the old days when the Hermit of Chappaqua was celebrated as the smartest woman in the world by the ABCCBSNBCCNNMSNBCPBS Cartel there was a joke that made the rounds:

Bill and Hillary pulled into a gas station in rural Arkansas and good old Bubba comes out to pump the gas. As he's wiping the windshield he looks through the glass and then says, "Hillary is that you?" It turns out that Hillary and Bubba used to date. As they pulled away America's most beloved sexual predator is laughing. Hillary asks, "Bill what's so funny?" The Prince of Interns says, "Here you are married to the President of the United States instead of married to some gas station attendant." Where upon Hillary quips, "Bill, if I would've married him he'd be the President of the United States."

A sequel to this apocryphal story could be:

Drain the Swamp

The two heads of New York's Sixth Crime Family are sitting at the inauguration of Donald Trump. Hillary says to Bill, "If it hadn't been for you and all your baggage that would be me up there." Bill leans over and whispers, "If you would have listened to me and campaigned instead of waiting to be crowned that might have been you up there."

Hillary ran an abysmal campaign. I haven't seen anything like it since Bob Dole ran on the logic of, "It's my turn."

Although some of us saw the coming collapse of the PC America Last crowd in the growing disgust of hard working Americans the central planners never did. They dismissed us as deplorable Bible clutching flag waving knuckle dragging tax paying bumpkins who lived in fly over country and could safely be ignored by our betters. They have come to rue the hubris of their assumption. They still don't get it, but they rue it, and to them ruing is a new experience.

So their chosen successor to the Great Apologizer fell flat on her pants suit and they don't know what to do. It couldn't have been that people actually rejected their plan to convert America into a third world hellhole one vote among many in a UN controlled New World Order. No, that couldn't be it. There must have been a conspiracy. So today we wander endlessly day and night through the twenty-four hour wall-to-wall fake news cycle of the Russians did it while trumpeting that Hillary won the popular vote. Now we learn when President Trump tweeted that he and his transition team were under surveillance by the Obama administration he was pointing to where the hacking may have all originated. Even a celebrated left winger like Oliver Stone on CNN as reported by the Daily Beast says the DNC hack was an inside job.[73] Another left leaning news source, Salon reports that our own intelligence agencies can hack sites and

---

[73] Wilstein, Matt, *The Daily Beast*, 4-13-17, accessed 6-16-19, https://www.thedailybeast.com/cheats/2016/09/13/oliver-stone-dnc-hack-was-an-inside-job-not-russia?source=copyurl&via=desktop

make it look like the Russians did it.[74] If possible a shadowy tale gets darker.

Susan Rice, President Obama's national-security adviser and confidant, called for American citizens who happened to be involved in the Trump campaign and transition team to be unmasked.[75] Then we learn that Evelyn Farkas, deputy assistant secretary of defense under Obama, has acknowledged efforts by her colleagues to gather intelligence on Trump team ties to Russia before Donald Trump took office and to conceal the sources of that intelligence from the incoming administration.[76] This isn't a smoking gun. It's two smoking guns. Both of these women need to testify

---

[74] Ryan, Danielle, *Salon*, 3-12-17, accessed 6-16-19, https://www.salon.com/2017/03/12/wikileaks-cia-dump-makes-the-russian-hacking-story-even-murkier-if-thats-possible/

[75] McCarthy, Andrew, *National Review*, 4-4-17, accessed 6-16-19, https://www.nationalreview.com/2017/04/susan-rice-unmasking-trump-campaign-members-obama-administration-fbi-cia-nsa/

[76] Kerwick, Jack, *Townhall*, 4-2-17, accessed 6-16-19, https://townhall.com/columnists/jackkerwick/2017/04/02/evelyn-farkass-six-revelations-about-obama-trump-and-the-deep-state-n2307464

under oath. Where's Trey Gowdy when you need him?

And yet, the beat goes on. It reminds me that the last person elected saying that he was going to drain the swamp was Richard Nixon in 1972. Before that it was JFK. It is obvious the Progressives are plotting the Nixon treatment for Mr. Trump. Let us pray no one attempts the JFK solution to their problem.

I might have just certified my induction into the Conspiracy Theorists Secret Handshake Society as far as any supporters of the establishment are concerned; however, I believe that the permanent government, now called the Deep State, has its own agenda and they are not above staging a silent coup to reign in any elected officials who get in the way.

Facts can be ignored:

Hillary won the popular vote

The Clintons have deep and long ties to Russian Oligarchs.[77]

The Clintons received millions from the Russians during the Uranium Deal.[78]

All those suspicious donations that we were assured weren't bribes dried up and the Clinton foundation is blowing away after Hillary lost the election.[79]

Obama administration officials broke the spirit and possibly the letter of the law in their attempts[80] to sabotage[81] the incoming Trump Administration.

---

[77] Sainto, Michael, *The Observer*, 3-23-17, accessed 6-16-19

[78] Becker, J., M., *The New York Times*, 3-23-15, accessed 6-16-19

[79] Fox News, 1-16-17, accessed 6-16-19, https://www.foxnews.com/politics/clinton-global-initiative-to-lay-off-employees-shut-down-amid-dwindling-donations

[80] Ross, C,, *The Daily Caller*, 3-1-17, accessed 6-16-19, https://dailycaller.com/2017/03/01/confirmed-obama-sabotaged-trumps-transition-to-the-white-house/

[81] Buchanan, P., *Townhall*, 3-24-17, accessed, https://townhall.com/columnists/patbuchanan/2017/03/24/the-obama-plot-to-sabotage-trump-n2303413

Not only does the media cartel put everything through their progressive spin cycle, if anything is reported that disrupts their playbook they go so far as to instruct their viewers to ignore the story.[82] What is so sad about this is that so many we know and love, those who get their personal opinion from the Cartel will do what they are instructed to do. They will ignore the facts and believe the lie.

Every conversation and keystroke recorded, cameras everywhere, investigations that have predetermined conclusions, and hearings that can only be seen as show trials and political theater that is America today. So if our government is watching everyone and editing the tapes here's my question: is anyone watching those who watch us? If you are don't tell anyone. It might be treason.

---

[82] Elliot, T., *grabienews*, 4-4-17, accessed 6-16-19, https://news.grabien.com/story-cnn-goes-rampage-against-susan-rice-bombshell-instructs-view

Dispatch Twelve

Are Democrats Smarter Than Republicans?

I have asked myself this question many times. Have recent events changed my mind?

The headline blares, "Nunes steps aside from Russia probe." Why? As Nunes puts it, "Several leftwing activist groups have filed accusations against me with the Office of Congressional Ethics. The charges are entirely false and politically motivated, and are being leveled just as the American people are beginning to learn the truth about the improper unmasking of the identities of U.S. citizens and other abuses of power."[83]

---

[83] Bresnahan, J, & Dawsey, J., *Politico*, 4-6-17, accessed 6-17, https://www.politico.com/story/2017/04/nunes-to-step-aside-from-russia-probe-236951

Do you think if this was House Intelligence Committee Vice Chairman Democrat Adam Schiff serving as the head of the committee he would step aside?[84] No way. If this was going on against a Democrat the entire Progressive establishment would be attacking the Ethics Committee for even accepting such accusations.

In a second example let's look at the Attorney General, Jeff Sessions. He recuses himself from the Russian witch hunt over non-issues.[85] Does anyone remember that Obama's last AG Loretta Lynch meeting with Ex-President Clinton on an airport in Arizona while her department was conducting a criminal investigation of his wife? Did she recuse herself? Of course not only Republicans are held to those standards.

Or look at the fake news tsunami about Russian meddling in our recent election.

---

[84] Rogers, A., CNN, 4-10-17, accessed, https://www.cnn.com/2017/04/07/opinions/nunes-departure-committee-forward-opinion-rogers/

[85] Landler, M. & Lichtblau, E., *New York Time*, 3-2-17, accessed, https://www.nytimes.com/2017/03/02/us/politics/jeff-sessions-russia-trump-investigation-democrats.html

After all this inquiry there is no evidence to support it. WIKI Leaks has provided documents that show our own intelligence organizations routinely hack computers and make it look like the Russians did it.[86] And besides as I have been pointing out all along if the Russians did hack the election and Hillary won the popular vote who was the recipient of any Russian help? Now it comes out that President Obama's political hatchet woman Susan Rice was the one unmasking people from the Trump campaign and transition team in broad sweep intel gatherings. So it looks like if any government was trying to interfere in a fair election it was ours.

And yet the media drum beat and the hearings, investigations, and charges continue. If this was happening to a Democrat, say to President Obama what would we hear? The media megaphone would be blaring day and night that it was a racially motivated witch hunt. And unlike the Republicans who have some of the

---

[86] *World Net Daily*, 3-7-17, accessed 6-17-19, https://www.wnd.com/2017/03/shocker-cia-can-mimic-russian-cyber-hack/

leaders of their party in and out of government and those in the media joining in the attacks in a similar situation the Democrats would circle the wagons and defend the attacked 24/7.

Like Charley Brown trying to kick the football over and over again only to have Lucy pull it away; each time the Democrats keep running the same play and the Republicans keep falling for it. This brings us to the question of the day, "Are Democrats smarter than Republicans?"

I was a fourth generation Republican who cut my teeth in Nixon's first presidential campaign back in 1960 and then in Barry Goldwater's failed Presidential bid. I worked for Goldwater, Reagan, and all the following Republican flag wavers who tried to rally the country to a return to limited government, personal liberty, and economic freedom. That is I did until Trent Lott's Republican Senate Majority gave us the impeachment debacle[87] and the explosion of

---

[87] Baker, P., Dewar, H., *The Washington Post*, 2-13-17, accessed 6-17-19, https://www.washingtonpost.com/wp-

government growth and spending[88] under Hastert, Lott, and Bush. When the Republican Senate refused to impeach President Clinton for crimes he later admitted and when they and their House brethren became Democrat Lite as the party of power, I mailed my membership card to the party that was no longer the Grand Old Party of my great grandfather and became an Independent.

For most of my life I was a party man: accepting some things I didn't agree with for the greater good of electing a party with a platform I could agree with. However, once it became apparent that as far as the budget went we had elected the foxes to watch the hen house, that the conservative social agenda received a tip-of-the-hat during elections followed by no action, and that the only victims of the impeachment were those brave enough to bring the charges the scales fell from my eyes. Once

---

srv/politics/special/clinton/stories/impeach021399.htm

[88] Independent Institute, accessed 6-17-19, http://www.independent.org/news/news_detail.asp?newsid=31

Drain the Swamp

I saw that the Republicans had lost their moorings and were swilling at the public trough, I realized the platform we conservatives battle so hard for and hold so dear is merely a mirage held in front of social and fiscal conservatives to keep them loyal to a Party captured by the Progressives.

Back in the Dream Time, when my mind was still locked in the glow of Ronald Reagan and all his example and message meant to America, even then I wondered, "What's wrong with these leaders of ours? Why do the Democrats always seem to outsmart them at every turn?"

Even Reagan, the best of the best, was hoodwinked by Tip O'Neal in the amnesty bargain: we would grant amnesty and then seal the border. The problem is the illegal immigrants got the amnesty; however, America's border was never sealed. He also signed several tax deals with the Democratic majority. *We the People* lost many deductions in exchange for lower rates. The deductions never came back even though the rates started rising again as soon as the Gipper said good night and George the First forgot to read his own lips.

George Bush the Elder was out maneuvered by the Progressives so many times that 20% of his base ran to Perot opening the door for Clinton and the first attempt to ram national health care down America's throat. That time they overplayed their hand and the last great strategist among the Republicans, Newt Gingrich was able to sell a Contract with America and bring the first Republican majority in Congress in 40 years.

Newt kept the promises and brought some fiscal sanity back to Washington. Within a few short years the Republican led Congress ended welfare as we had known it for generations and balanced the budget. Unfortunately the Party of Lincoln then nominated someone who campaigned as if he had voted for Lincoln. The 1996 Republican campaign would have had to improve several thousand percent to make it to dull. Suddenly, with an assist from the Corporations Once Known as the Mainstream Media it was Clinton, who had been dragged kicking and screaming to the benefit and spending cutting table, who was the author of everything positive Congress had accomplished. The Republicans had been outmaneuvered and outsmarted again.

According to every one of the serial recounts Bush the younger won Florida and legitimately the presidential race of 2000. Yet, to this day people talk of him being selected not elected. After the dastardly deeds of 9-11 the rhetorically-challenged George captured the hearts of America and the admiration of the Western world by taking a bullhorn and talking to a crowd at ground zero. Yet by fighting and winning America's first preemptive war and then losing the peace through the lack of planning he soon lost the PR campaign which led to the Pelosi-Reid Congress in 2006 and eventually to the absolute triumph of Progressivism in 2008.

Once their secular messiah was enthroned at 1600 Pennsylvania Avenue the Progressives with their filibuster proof majority took the reins of single-party rule and imposed their radical agenda to transform America into a Nanny-state based upon the re-distribution of wealth. This wanton destruction of the traditional American society based on limited government and free enterprise sparked a vast rebellion of the silent majority resulting in the teanami of 2010[89] which brought a Republican majority back to the People's House and an expanded minority to the Senate.

And what is the first thing these political savants do? They reaffirm the same tired leadership and strike a deal[90] that anyone who was paying attention could see was tailor made to save the discredited Obama presidency and set the stage for him to follow in Mr. Clinton's footsteps taking credit for anything good the historic election might have made possible. What were these so-called leaders thinking? They turned the

---

[89] Owen, C., *The Christian Science Monitor,* 11-3-10, accessed 6-17-19, https://www.csmonitor.com/USA/Elections/2010/1103/After-GOP-landslide-of-Election-2010-what-next-for-Obama
[90] Morrissey, E., *Hot Air,* 4-14-11, accessed 6-17-19, https://hotair.com/archives/2011/04/14/how-bad-was-the-budget-deal-actually/

victory of the grassroots into a capitulation to the elites. Not only did they sign a deal that extended uncertainty and raised estate taxes, they gave the Administration cover for a stealth stimulus filled with porkulous pay-offs designed to help re-elect the President.

Along comes 2012 and the Republican establishment and their friends in the Progressive Media engineer the nomination of the one man who couldn't beat the worst president in American History with the worst economy since 1932. They surrender the issue of a massively unpopular Obamacare by nominating the author of its prototype. Mr. Romney spends the last debate agreeing with the President's handling of foreign policy and ignoring the raging controversy over the debacle in Benghazi.[91] If he didn't throw the election he tossed it away.

Then came Trump, he wins fair and square yet he is illegitimate. There is no evidence

[91] *The Week*, 10-22-12, accessed 6-17-19, https://theweek.com/articles/471161/final-presidential-debate-does-mitt-romney-agree-obama-foreign-policy

of any collusion with the Russians but the seriousness of the charges demand an investigation as is the Democrat standard operating procedure. All of this smoke and mirrors might easily be a cover so that no one gets to investigate the real scandal, that the Obama administration spied on and distributed the findings in an attempt to sabotage the incoming Trump. And the Republicans are either right in there working with the Democrats, they recuse themselves, or they're merely ineffective in dispersing the smoke and revealing the truth.

So, "Are Democrats smarter than Republicans?" The answer is they aren't. It isn't a matter of intelligence it's a matter of people with dedication to something larger than themselves, as opposed to people with dedication to seeing themselves as something larger than they are.

The leadership of the Democrat Party is composed of committed radical Progressives. They have a long term agenda to transform America into a socialist welfare state with an unlimited government, and they never lose sight of that goal. They're willing to commit political suicide, or more accurately they're willing to encourage their follow travelers who do not occupy safe seats to commit political suicide usually with pay off jobs in government agencies. They never take their eyes off the ball. They're constantly pushing to move closer to the goal line even if it's one inch at a time. And after the debacle that was Hillary they are warming[92] to the idea of allowing an outright Socialist to become the leader and agenda driver of their Party.[93]

They say a leopard can't change his spots and at least the sheep's clothing is falling off the Faux Socialists who call themselves Democrats. It is interesting to remember that the Communist Party USA went all in

---

[92] Levitz, E., *The Intelligencer*, 4-3-17, accessed 6-17-19,
http://nymag.com/intelligencer/2017/04/congressional-democrats-warm-to-bernie-sanderss-agenda.html?gtm=bottom
[93] Bunker, T., *Newsmax*, 4-17-17, accessed 6-17-19,
http://nymag.com/intelligencer/2017/04/congressional-democrats-warm-to-bernie-sanderss-agenda.html?gtm=bottom

for Obama and Clinton.[94] Why run your own candidate when one of the major parties is doing it for you. These are some dedicated community organizers who aim at nothing less than fundamentally transforming America.

By comparison, the leadership of the Republicans is composed of professional politicians. They're pragmatists who do whatever they have to do and say whatever they have to say to retain their seats, their power, and their perks. They believe the inside the beltway press who tell them how visionary they are to compromise, losing sight of those back home in fly-over country who instead believed the campaign promises and expect their representatives to stand up for principles.

The Party of Lincoln over-and-over chooses to be on the receiving end of Pickett's Charge instead of behind the spit-rail fence firing point blank as their enemy wastes itself in a senseless assault against an

[94] Duke, S., *New American*, 8-10-16, accessed 6-17-19,
https://www.thenewamerican.com/usnews/politics/item/23834-communist-party-goes-all-in-for-hillary

immovable barrier. The Republicans control the House, the Senate, and the Presidency. They could be that immovable barrier holding back the advancing forces of bankruptcy and collapse. Instead the Progressives of the right are once again embracing the frivolous and spurious attacks of the Left against anyone who is really trying to lead away from the super state. Soon they will join the Progressives of left in a bi-partisan campaign to continue the spending, increase the debt, and fool the public.

Paraphrasing the first Republican President, Historian Will Durant once wisely observed, "It may be true that you can't fool all the people all the time, but you can fool enough of them to rule a large country."[95]

Looking at the question which is the title of this essay, "Are Democrats smarter than Republicans" over many years of pondering this question, I haven't changed my mind. Singleness of purpose and focusing on a goal will make one appear smarter than

---

[95] Brainy Quotes, accessed 6-17-19, https://www.brainyquote.com/authors/will_durant

someone who is merely in it for what they can get. In other words, people who are dedicated to achieving long-term goals who have the ability to delay gratification will always trump self-serving pragmatists who can see no further than the feathers in their own nest.

Drain the Swamp

Dispatch Thirteen

War Does Not Bring Peace

I am a supporter of our troops. I believe they are patriots and America's best. I don't question the bravery or skill of our troops it's the imperial foreign policy which sends them as sacrifices on the altar of political ambition that I question.

The cruel calculations of political elites using our service men and women as pawns on their partisan game board are shameful. The most shocking example of this was President Obama announcing a surge in troops at the same time he announced the exit strategy for leaving the country.[96] What could be more counterproductive than

---

[96] *The Wall Street Journal*, 12-1-09, accessed 6-17-19, https://www.wsj.com/video/obama-announces-troop-surge-and-withdrawal-plans/55DC120D-6501-4042-B861-50513E703E38.html

telling an asymmetrical enemy, "If you hang on long enough we leave and you win."

Look at Iraq. We went to war to stop the spread of weapons of mass destruction which even President Bush eventually admitted were never there.[97] We went to war because our leaders intimated that Iraq had a hand in the sneak attacks of 9-11 based on a rumored meeting between an Iraqi agent and Mohamed Atta another claim that has since been repudiated.[98] Did we go to war to correct the partial victory we gained in Gulf War I under George I? Did we go to war as George II later claimed to make the Mideast safe for democracy? Whatever the reason for invading Iraq, a nation we supported for years, a nation which had not and was not planning to attack us, what did we accomplish and what do we have now that we are gone?

What about Afghanistan? After the sneak attacks on 9-11 we had every legal and

---

[97] *Divergence and Convergence*, 11-2-10, accessed 6-17-19, http://divergence-convergence.blogspot.com/2010/11/bush-admits-iraq-had-no-weapons-of-mass.html
[98] Ibid.

moral right to attack the nation that harbored and protected Al-Qaeda. The whole world supported our right to punish those who had so cruelly attacked us.

However, to keep faith with the Constitution a declaration of war should have been obtained. Instead we followed the pattern of all military actions since WW II a guns and butter approach where war is waged off somewhere in the distance. It is shielded by a compliant media and the fog of official pronouncements so our elites can keep the political landscape manageable at home.

Our armed forces waged a brilliant campaign that dismantled the Taliban regime in short order. Then instead of saying, "If it happens again we'll come back again," and leaving we have stayed for more than a dozen years squandering hundreds of billions building a nation for people who don't see themselves as a nation. They are a collection of tribes grouped together by the necessities of international politics surrounded by a porous border and a history of ungovernable conflict.

Does anyone doubt that after we leave Kabul the Taliban will return? Does anyone doubt that the training and weapons that we have given to our Afghan allies which are turned against us on a regular basis will form the bedrock of future Taliban strength? Does anyone doubt that as we roll out the front door our Afghan puppets will be taking 747s filled with their plunder of American taxpayer cash on their way to a luxurious exile at our expense?

The Constitution gives Congress the exclusive right to declare war. This limitation on the prerogative of our chief executive to commit America to war without the consent of the citizens was considered one of the most important strengths of the document. The founders of our nation came from a society in which autocratic kings had often plunged their nations into wars based on their own desires, whims, and political machinations. Those who wrote the Constitution to be the framework for a new type of nation determined that we should never go to war unless it was the expression of the people through their elected representatives. They believed this

would limit war to the defense of the
Republic and its vital interests.

There hasn't been a declared war since
World War II and yet our sons and
daughters have fought and died in countless
battles around the world. With the war in
Afghanistan winding up and down the
Neocons and Progressives are beating the
war drums daily for intervention in North
Korea, Syria, Iran, and even war with
Russia and China.

The Obama Administration's policy of
supporting Islamic Radicals, supplied
weapons to the Al-Qaeda led Syrian rebels
for years. I contend the Mission in Benghazi
and its satellite CIA Safe-House was in
reality a conduit for transferring untraceable
weapons from the captured Libyan arsenal
through Turkey to the rebels.[99] So when it
comes to Syria we are already there and we
have been since the beginning. We have
had Special Forces on the ground. We have
trained so-called moderate Islamists who to

---

[99] *National Review*, 8-2-19, accessed 6-17-19,
https://www.nationalreview.com/2016/08/hillary-
clinton-wikileaks-benghazi-scandal-arm-syrian-
rebels-al-qaeda-isis-libya-turkey/

a man have taken the training and weapons to ISIS as quickly as they could.[100] Now our Neo-con cheerleaders want us to directly intervene.[101]

The same goes for Iran. There is a shadow war that has been raging for years between Israel with American support and Iran.[102] This shadow war consists of assassinations of nuclear scientists, bombing nuclear facilities and uploading computer viruses into computers used to control the cyclotrons used to enrich uranium on the part of the allies. The response has been attacks against Israeli citizens around the world and even a bombing attempt in Washington D.C.

---

[100] Klein, A., *World Net Daily*, 6-17-14, accessed 6-17-19, https://www.wnd.com/2014/06/officials-u-s-trained-isis-at-secret-base-in-jordan/

[101] Madams, D., Ron Paul Institute, 2-1-17, Accessed 6-17-19, http://www.ronpaulinstitute.org/archives/peace-and-prosperity/2017/february/01/war-drums-trumps-national-security-advisor-threatens-iran/

[102] Taylor, G., *The Washington Times*, 3-19-13, accessed 6-17-19, https://www.washingtontimes.com/news/2013/mar/19/shadow-war-between-israel-iran-rages-on-as-obama-v/?utm_source=RSS_Feed&utm_medium=RSS

This was not enough. America was been goaded into imposing draconian sanctions against Iran. Sanctions which if imposed on us we would be consider acts of war.[103] Once again this was not enough. The Neocons were working day and night to get us to deliver some shock and awe all over Iran all in the name of peace. The Iran deal paying off the Ayatollahs may have pushed this brewing confrontation to the back burner but make no mistake McCain and Company still have their cross hairs trained on Tehran.

Iran has not attacked another country in the memory of anyone who is alive today. Or in the lives of the ancestors going back hundreds of years. America's intelligence agencies unanimously tell us, Congress, and the Administration that Iran does not have a nuclear weapons program.[104] Iran is a signer of the Nuclear Proliferation Treaty, and as a part of that treaty it is guaranteed

---

[103] RT, 2-19-12, accessed 6-17-19, https://www.rt.com/news/iran-us-sanctions-war-677/

[104] Dilliania, K., *The Los Angeles Times*, 2-23-12, accessed https://www.latimes.com/archives/la-xpm-2012-feb-23-la-fg-iran-intel-20120224-story.html

the right to develop nuclear power for peaceful means and we have no proof that they are doing anything else. In other words we have paid them hundreds of billions to stop doing something our own intelligence services say they weren't doing.

As far as Iran is concerned we were told "Containment is off the table."[105] Now we are told "All options are on the table." Why was containment off the table? It worked during the Cold war when we faced off with an enemy many times larger with thousands of nuclear weapons on delivery systems aimed at our cities. Why won't it work against a nation that at this point has no nuclear weapons?

Why was it acceptable for North Korea to have nuclear weapons but not Iran? Does anyone think the Ayatollahs are crazier than the boy dictator of the Kim dynasty? There is no doubt that the United States military has the ability to destroy Iran's conventional defensive and offensive resources within a short time.

[105105] *Capitol Hill Blue*, 11-6-10, accessed 6-17-19, https://www.capitolhillblue.com/node/34848

Drain the Swamp

It is obvious we could, "Bomb them both back to the stone age" as the saying goes. However that wouldn't necessarily mean that some of the stones thrown later in the contest might not hurt. Iran and North Korea both have unknown asymmetrical war capabilities.

It's believed that their allies in Gaza and Lebanon would immediately attack Israel. The Iranians would also do all they could to interrupt the supply of the oil upon which we continue to allow ourselves to depend. They would attempt to attack the oil fields of their neighbors, to close the Straits of Hormuz, attack nearby American bases, and possible stir up rebellions in Sunni ruled countries with either sizable Shiite minorities or in some cases majorities.

North Korea would immediately shell Seoul and inflict per4haps millions of casualties. Our troops, over 20,000 strong are right in the line of fire. Their massive wall of artillery is protected by sophisticated SAM sites that would exact a high price from our Air Force. And with a million man army of fanatic loyalists a land invasion would be daunting to say the least.

We might even face terrorist attacks here in the Homeland. This war would not be a cake walk. The military and economic consequences would be immediate and they would be dire.

However, as dire as these consequences would be these are not potentially the most troubling. War opens the door for domestic changes that would not be possible during normal times. While we have been and are engaged in a multi-generational seemingly endless series of wars this war might be different. While all our other wars have been fought over there the civilian population continued to live as if Americans were not in harm's way even though they were. In other words we managed to have both guns and butter, war overseas and peace at home. In the case of a war with Iran, North Korea, Russia, or China we might face a situation that could bring the war home to America in multiple ways.

Economically gas could skyrocket causing dislocation in our fragile economy. On the military front terror sleeper cells could be activated in America or terrorists could come in through our porous borders. Both the economic impact and terrorist activities would open the door for drastic government action which could well negatively impact our lives. Rights are often curtailed in times of emergency. The cost of war is often seen in the growth of government power and the loss of freedom at home. We might even have to institute a military draft. Does anyone think the snowflake generation would meekly march off to boot camp? Does anyone think they might melt at the first day in boot camp? "Where are our safe zones?" "I should be in the WACS!" "The drill sergeant looked at me and now I feel threatened."

Our worldwide military presence is not keeping us safe and in many ways it's provocative. Peace and equitable trade with all is the course recommended by our founders. It was the foreign policy of every administration until McKinley and the default position until FDR. Let us return to our traditions and reject these endless wars for peace. Let us quit supporting other economies with our foreign bases. Let us end the many entangling agreements that bind us to fight for others who should instead fight for themselves.

With real peace we could perhaps deal with the domestic issues that are tearing us apart and driving us into bankruptcy. Every patriot should recognize the danger new fronts in our never-ending war will have on our current battle to maintain personal liberty, individual freedom, and economic opportunity here at home. Consequently patriots should do everything in their power to stop the stampede to war. Stand up for real peace and not for more wars for a peace that never comes. No matter how they package it war does not bring peace.

Drain the Swamp

Dispatch Fourteen

Republican Strategy: Retreat From Victory

Having won the white House, the House,
and the Senate the victorious Republicans
have handed the Democrats the budget
process. In doing so they have surrendered
everything they were supposedly fighting
for: no wall, no end to Obamacare, no end
to sanctuary cities, and no end to funding
for Planned Parenthood. The Democrat
leaders are celebrating their victory after
losing election after election. Those of us
who voted Republican, who voted to get our
country back, are mourning a loss after
winning election after election. This does
not bode well for the Republican Party, the
democratic process, or the social contract in
America.

I once asked the question: are Democrats
smarter than Republicans. Just asking the

113

question enraged many of the "Read the headline and ignore the article" crowd. If they had read the article they would have learned that my answer to that question was no, they aren't smarter just dedicated to a larger purpose than feathering their own nests or maintaining power.

The Democrats of today present a unified front dedicated to transforming America into the Progressive dream / the American nightmare of a collectivized state.

The Republicans, after having been co-opted and led by Progressives calling themselves Republicans for the past twenty years, are struggling through the Trump Revolution. The same congressional leaders are still in place: Ryan, McConnell, McCain, etc. and they are as intent on obstructing the President as their colleagues Schumer and Pelosi.

Don't be fooled by the label Republican. What President Trump is facing is a twin headed bird of prey; the Republicrat government party. This self-serving combination is the political expression of their philosophical mentors in academia. They receive their marching orders daily through the megaphone provided by the Corporations Once Known as the Mainstream Media. They apply social pressure in the streets through their bully-boys the Anti-Fa bandanna wearing thugs who use violence to shut down free speech.

Where is this headed?

I believe that at some point the House will begin impeachment hearings. The Media will of course continue their feeding frenzy of Anti-Trump hysteria. The Bully-boys will try to stifle anyone who disagrees. The usual suspects will follow their philosophical leader, Maxine Waters, into the streets and the fake news media will do their best to make it appear that the whole country wants their coup to succeed.

Washington has spent generations trying to make everyone believe that only the technicians of the political maze are qualified to steer the Ship of State. In reality the first 535 names in the phone book could probably do as well and at least we would have some regular people in there and maybe some common sense.

Drain the Swamp

So far they've used the courts, the Congress, the bureaucracy, and the media to block and demean everything President Trump tries to do, everything we elected him to do. If they manage to overthrow the results of the election in another silent coup we may witness the final unraveling of the social contract in America.

For years the Republicans chased votes by saying, "Give us the power and we will right the Ship of State." We gave them the House. They said they needed the Senate too before they could do anything. We gave them the Senate. Then they said they also needed the White House before they could do anything. We gave them the White House. And what do we get? A retreat from victory. Now they say, "Wait till September." Personally I don't think I'll hold my breath.

This budget surrender is a betrayal. The legal contortions of the judiciary are shameful. The unhinged media assault is transparent. And any attempt to overthrow this president may well be suicidal.

Drain the Swamp

Dispatch Fifteen

Torpedoes Sink Ships

Ships of State that is.

Once wars made presidents popular. Think of Washington and the Revolution, Lincoln and the Civil War, McKinley and the Spanish American War, FDR and WW II. Maybe that was because we used to win wars.

Korea ran Truman out of office. Vietnam made LBJ decide not to run. Before the Silent Coup, Nixon (who ended the war) was tarred with the Vietnam brush. With America winning once again, George the First got a bump from the 100 day Gulf One before we all read his lips. Then rounding out the results of quagmire wars George the Second after soaring in the aftermath of 9-11 ran aground on the sand bars of Iraq.

I am a non-interventionist. I believe in America First. I support the foreign policy of Thomas Jefferson, "Peace, commerce and honest friendship with all nations; entangling alliances with none."[106]

We don't need to intervene in the wars of others. We don't need to fight proxy wars in foreign lands. We don't need to crusade our way into a religious war with over a billion people.

We have a war right here, the Culture War long ago defined by the prescient ideological father of the Trump Revolution, Pat Buchanan at the 1992 Republican Convention when he said, "There is a religious war going on in this country. It is a cultural war, as critical to the kind of nation we shall be as was the Cold War itself, for this war is for the soul of America."[107]

The Progressives of the Obamanation, their Clintonian allies in New York's Sixth Crime Family, and the Sandersnista Antifa Black Shirts have been stalled in their Long March

---

[106] Brainyquotes, accessed 6-18-19, https://www.brainyquote.com/quotes/thomas_jefferson_157206
[107] *Voices of Democracy*, accessed 6-18-19, http://voicesofdemocracy.umd.edu/buchanan-culture-war-speech-speech-text/

to a socialist America by the Trump phenomenon. Daily the ABCCBSNBCCNNMSNBCPBS Cartel hammers away in their effort to de-legitimize President Trump. The low information voters who get their personal opinions from the Democrat stenographers in the Cartel repeat the talking points released by Schumer, Pelosi, and the Deep State. The RINOs following McCain are yearning to stretch their hands across the aisles doing anything they can to embarrass or undermine President Trump.

The neo-con dream weavers are working day and night to lure Mr. Trump into a foreign adventure. If they can somehow get a war started that they can hang around his neck the miracle election may fizzle into the counter-revolution of a midterm election debacle and the inevitable impeachment hearings that would bring.

Instead of following the McCain/Krauthammer/Crystal wing to war somewhere for something lets quit subsidizing the economies of over a hundred countries with our bases. Bring our troops home let them build the wall and secure our own borders. Build the most sophisticated and powerful defenses imagined and defend America First.

An American hero once said, "Damn the torpedoes, full speed ahead!"[108] The torpedoes of war often sink the ship of state. Even the victorious often fall victim to the terminal bleeding of a Pyrrhic victory.[109] Look at Britain. They lost two generations to win two world wars and the empire they fought to save died from the wounds.

Mr. President I know the pressure to go to war is mounting. To take a battle cry from the dis-loyal opposition, "Resist!" Defend us if we are attacked. Build the Wall. Secure the border. Win the war at home don't be sidetracked into the abyss that has swallowed other presidencies. We won the wars in Afghanistan and Iraq and then the

---

[108] History, accessed 6-18-19, https://www.history.com/topics/american-civil-war/david-farragut
[109] Cambridge Dictionary, accessed 6-18-19, https://dictionary.cambridge.org/us/dictionary/english/pyrrhic-victory

protracted nation-building melted the consensus of world support we received after 9-11. To many around the world and here at home we have become the aggressors. Look what it did to the approval rating for George the Second.

War always leads to destruction. It's supposed to. Since Truman invented the idea of limited war even the victories have felt more like defeats. Look at Vietnam. Mr. President you were elected by people who want secure borders, a rebirth of American industry, and a return to the fundamentals of the American Experiment; limited government, personal liberty, and economic opportunity. Don't fall into the trap of a foreign war. Win the war at home instead.

Dispatch Sixteen

They Serve at the Pleasure of the President

How does impeachment of a president work? The House of Representatives acting as a super grand jury votes an indictment or impeachment. The Senate acting as a jury decides whether or not the charges brought warrant conviction. If the president is convicted by the Senate he is removed from office. If two thirds of the Senate fails to vote to convict the charges are dropped. In that case the president was still impeached but not convicted.

In 1868 the House of Representatives voted to impeach President Andrew Johnson. This was the first time any president was impeached. Contrary to popular belief President Nixon was never impeached. He resigned while the Watergate debacle was still under investigation. President Clinton was impeached but like Johnson he was not convicted by the Senate so he remained in office until the end of his term.

Why is this history lesson appropriate for May 17, 2017? Because I believe President Trump is going to be impeached.

Why was Andrew Johnson impeached? Although there were eleven articles of impeachment the main reason and primary cause was that he fired Edwin M. Stanton from the office of Secretary of the Department of War. Congress had passed a law: the Tenure of Office Act. This became law in 1867, over the veto of President Andrew Johnson. It denied the president the power to remove any executive officer who had been appointed by the president with the advice and consent of the Senate, unless the Senate approved the removal during the next full session of Congress. The act was significantly amended on April 5, 1869. Congress repealed the act in its entirety in 1887. In 1926, the Supreme Court ruled that it was unconstitutional even though it had been repealed almost forty years before.

All appointees of the executive office serve at the pleasure of the president. He hires them, and even though the major ones must be confirmed by the Senate, he can fire them.

Andrew Johnson missed being convicted by the Senate by one vote.

Why was Bill Clinton impeached? In this case there were only two articles of impeachment: lying under oath to a federal grand jury and obstructing justice. President Clinton was acquitted on both articles of impeachment. Needing a two-thirds majority to convict the prosecution failed to achieve even a majority. On the first charge of perjury, 45 Democrats and 10 Republicans voted "not guilty," and on the second charge of obstruction of justice the Senate was split 50-50. However, others who were not as politically attuned were not so lenient.

In April 1999, U.S. District Judge Susan Webber Wright found Clinton in contempt of court for giving false testimony in the Paula Jones sexual harassment trial and fined him more than $90,000.[110] Once he lost his presidential immunity he was disbarred from practicing law in Arkansas and was also disbarred from practicing law in front of the Supreme Court. Additionally he was fined $25,000 for his testimony in the Lewinsky incident.

Now the impeachment drums are beating again. Democrats determined since November 8th to declare the Trump victory illicit by any means necessary are planning a coup. The RESIST! Movement with its Antifa bully boys dressed in black hiding behind masks has no legs. The American people will tire of their over-the-top antics and eventually they will spawn their own backlash in a call for law and order.

However, the political hacks, the perpetually re-elected in Congress are a horse of different color. They're biding their time waiting for enough blood to stain the

---

[110] *The Guardian*, 10-1-01,accessed 6-18-19, https://www.theguardian.com/world/2001/oct/02/duncancampbell

water. They're waiting for their stenographers in the ABCCBSNBCPBSCNNMSNBC Cartel to give them enough political cover. Then they'll pounce.

Andrew Johnson was a Democrat impeached by a Republican Congress after the Civil War when the Democrat Party was completely discredited. The Republicans had a super majority and still they couldn't convict.

In Bill Clinton's case Republicans voted with Democrats not to convict even though some on both sides of the aisle gave speeches saying they knew he was guilty and repudiating his actions.

In the case of President Trump his political enemies have been field testing charges since day one. They say Russians hacked the election, and even though Hillary won the popular vote these hypothetical Russians were trying to elect Trump. They say President Trump colluded with the Russians to steal the election. Even though months of hearings and armies of investigative reporters have been chasing this mirage there is still no evidence.

Now he fired the Director of the FBI, and he supposedly gave classified information to the Russians. Everyone admits he has every right to fire any of the political appointees in the executive branch, and President Putin is offering to give the official transcripts of the meeting between Mr. Trump and the Russian ambassador which prove no classified information was shared. However innocence may not be enough to avoid impeachment just as it might not be enough to avoid conviction.

Why? Because the Ryan Rhinos control the house and the McCain/McConnell Never Trumpers control the Senate.

Donald Trump is the one thing none of the elites of the Washington Swamp can abide: a non-politician who beat them all at their own game. They cannot afford to let anyone see behind the curtain and find out how the sausage is made. They are dedicated to the proposition that government is too complicated for an average Joe to understand. While Mr. Trump is far from an average Joe he is not one of them. He didn't go to the right schools, he didn't pay his dues on the hustings, and he shines the light on the fact that they aren't as special as they want us to think they are.

As I have said many times, I think the first 535 names out of any phone book would yield a Congress at least as good as what we have. What we have now is the best Congress money can buy. Under the Telephone Book Party we would at least have a few regular people in there.

Watch the news. Try to discern the fake from the real. Tempests in teapots and phony scandals will continue to ruffle the waters until the Government Party is ready to overthrow the Country Party. I believe impeachment will come. What will be the reaction of those riding the Trump train?

Will it be despair and withdrawal or rage and confrontation?

Over the years I have offered one piece of advice repeatedly. Keep the faith. Keep the peace. We shall overcome.

Dispatch Seventeen

We Need More Special Counsels

The original accusation, the underlying premise for the entire hissy fit by the chronic sufferers of Trump Derangement Syndrome's about Russian collusion was that the Russians hacked the DNC and gave the emails to Wikileaks.

Recently Internet entrepreneur and hacker, Kim DotCom, admitted that he was part of an operation along with Seth Rich, an employee of the DNC to get internal emails to Wikileaks.[111]

Now we have proof that this underlying premise was a lie all along. We now know

---

[111] Hoft, J., *The Gateway Pundit*, 5-23-17, accessed 6-18-19, https://www.thegatewaypundit.com/2017/05/breaking-internet-hacker-kim-dot-com-releases-documents-seth-rich-leaked-podesta-wikileaks-emails/

that the person who really did give the DNC emails to Wikileaks didn't have to hack in, because he was an insider to begin with: Seth Rich.[112]

We also know that Seth Rich was mysteriously killed in Washington DC on July 8, 2016, 27 and that the Metro Police are slow walking the investigation.[113] The police say it was a botched robbery. The killer or killers took nothing from their victim, leaving behind his wallet, watch, and phone.

In August Wikileaks offered a $20,000 reward for information on the murder of DNC staffer Seth Rich. Julian Assange also suggested in August that Seth Rich was a Wikileaks informant. Kim Dotcom tweeted out that he has evidence Seth Rich, the murdered DNC operative, is the Wikileaks source.[114] He's ready to release the

---

[112] Ibid.

[113] Crokin, L., *World Net Daily*, 5-21-17, accessed 6-18-19, https://www.wnd.com/2017/05/bar-manager-cops-never-talked-with-staff-about-night-seth-rich-died/

[114] Hoft, J. 5-20-17, *Gateway Pundit*, accessed 6-18-19, https://www.thegatewaypundit.com/2017/05/boom-

evidence to Congressional investigators.[115] It doesn't seem as if anyone in Washington is interested since this shines a light on the lie that started it all.

There is so much about this that is interesting. Such as, the fact that the DNC leaders, Hillary Clinton, and Podesta, never disputed what was said in the emails. They instead attacked how the information was leaked. The media of course misdirected as best they could to cover up the facts. Look at who made the accusations not at the accusations themselves.

If there was any fraud in the last election cycle it was the DNC fat cats stacking the deck against Bernie Sanders in the primaries.

I continue to ask if the Russians hacked the election and Hillary won the popular vote whose side were they on. Just ask yourself: who would the Russians rather have as president of the United States a corrupt

---

hacker-kim-dotcom-knew-seth-rich-wikileaks-source-involved/
[115] Ibid.

politician that everyone in the world knows can be bribed or a billionaire who says, "Drill Baby drill" when their economy is based on oil?

Now we have a Special Counsel to investigate a non-crime that probably makes sense inside the beltway and through the looking glass.

Why not have a Special Counsel to investigate Bill Clinton's visit with Loretta Lynch on the tarmac in Arizona. How about one to investigate all the people illegally leaking confidential material in an attempt to thwart the Trump agenda? What about one to investigate how many people were illegally unmasked by Susan Rice and the rest of the Obama Hit machine?

If we're going to empanel Special Counsels to investigate rumors why stop until we've investigated them all?

Where are the over 30,000 emails deleted by Hillary Clinton?

If the massive donations to the Clinton Foundations weren't thinly veiled bribes why did they dry up as soon as Hillary lost the election?

Special Counsels like Special Prosecutors take on a life of their own. Which is eventually close to the half-life of a radioactive material, it lives on and on and on. They need convictions to justify the bloated staffs and budgets that they acquire in years of so-called investigations.

Look at the case of who leaked the name of Valerie Plame.[116] The whole thing started with an article on July 14, 2003, by Robert Novak, journalist for The Washington Post. This article named Plame as a CIA operative effectively ending her career. Before the Special Prosecutor was even named people in the government knew that the source of the leak was Richard Armitage. However he was an insider, a member of the establishment, so he couldn't end up as the fall guy.

---

[116] Hitchens, C. *Slate*, 8-29-06, accessed 6-18-19, https://slate.com/news-and-politics/2006/08/plamegate-s-ridiculous-conclusion.html

Drain the Swamp

Special Prosecutor Patrick Fitzgerald pushed and prodded until he was able to catch someone in a discrepancy between multiple interviews over several years. Then he prosecuted Scooter Libby for that discrepancy and got a conviction. It was not for revealing Plame's name but for impeding the investigation into something that was already known before the investigation began.

Back in 1980 when Ronald Reagan won shocking the Democrat establishment they demanded an investigation of his Presidential campaign saying they made a deal with Iran to delay the release of American hostages until after the election. How else could this has been actor beat a sitting president as successful as Jimmy Carter? That's when Tom Foley the Democrat leader of the House said, "We have no conclusive evidence of wrongdoing, but the seriousness of the allegations, and the weight of circumstantial information, compel an effort to establish the facts."[117] As long as we are going to continue to follow the Democrat's criteria for investigations let's go for the Holy Grail.

Let's investigate the report that Obama's Kenyan (paternal) grandmother, as well as his half-brother and half-sister testified that Barack Hussein Obama was born in Kenya, and not in Hawaii as the president claims.[118] And there is reported testimony from a Mombasa science teacher and the Mombasa Registrar of births that Obama's birth certificate from Mombasa is genuine. This report shows a copy of President Obama's birth certificate that Lucas Smith obtained through the help of a Kenyan Colonel who got it recently directly

---

[117] Berke, R., New York Times, 8-6-91, accessed 6-18-19,
https://www.nytimes.com/1991/08/06/us/inquiry-is-ordered-on-1980-campaign.html?pagewanted=all&mtrref=undefined&gwh=9041347C361BAAD7224EBBA904C8F90C&gwt=pay
[118] Yonah, T. Arutz Sheva 7, 12-10-08, accessed 6-18-19

from the Coast General Hospital in
Mombasa, Kenya.[119]

So, if we're going to have Special Counsels
let's have a bunch of them. Let's look into
every rumor and accusation in
Washington. That should cause enough
gridlock to hopefully protect us from all the
help the perpetually re-elected continue to
force upon us. Maybe then we could live
our lives in peace as they all scurry into the
shadows like roaches when you turn on the
light.

Drain the swamp!

---

[119] Rense.com, 1-31-19, accessed 6-18-19,
http://www.catholicbook.com/catholicbook/Obama%
20summary.htm

Drain the Swamp

Dispatch Eighteen

American Spy-Master
and Election Hacker Revealed

For months we've heard endless reports
concerning the supposed ties between the
Trump campaign and the Darth Vader of the
progressive's nightmares, Putin's Russia.
The thin gruel of this plot has swirled from
the swamp in DC through the megaphone of
the ABCCBSNBCPBSCNNMSNBC Cartel until
one would think every day Americans out
here in fly-over country were actually
thinking about it.

Finally after months of exhaustive research
the spy-master of the most extensive
surveillance campaign aimed at Americans
can be revealed. The one man who used
every avenue possible to invade the privacy
of American citizens in History has had the
mask of denial ripped away. Besides Hillary
and the DNC rigging the primaries to stop

Bernie who actually tried to use illegally obtained information to influence the presidential election in 2016?

The Obama Administration routinely spied on Americans. According to John Solomon and Sara Carter of CIRCA:

> The National Security Agency under former President Barack Obama routinely violated American privacy protections while scouring through overseas intercepts and failed to disclose the extent of the problems until the final days before Donald Trump was elected president last fall, according to once top-secret documents that chronicle some of the most serious constitutional abuses to date by the U.S. intelligence community.

> More than 5 percent, or one out of every 20 searches seeking upstream Internet data on Americans inside the NSA's so-called Section 702 database violated the safeguards Obama and his intelligence chiefs vowed to follow

in 2011, according to one classified internal report reviewed by Circa.

The Obama administration self-disclosed the problems at a closed-door hearing Oct. 26 before the Foreign Intelligence Surveillance Court that set off alarm. Trump was elected less than two weeks later.

The normally supportive court censured administration officials, saying the failure to disclose the extent of the violations earlier amounted to an "institutional lack of candor" and that the improper searches constituted a "very serious Fourth Amendment issue," according to a recently unsealed court document dated April 26, 2017.

The admitted violations undercut one of the primary defenses that the intelligence community and Obama officials have used in recent weeks to justify their snooping into incidental NSA intercepts about Americans.

According to Paul Sperry of the New York Post the Obama Admiration used its control of America's vast intelligence gathering apparatus in an attempt to hack the election.[120] While the show trials in Congress continue to build a paint-by-numbers PR case about Russians acting in collusion with the Trump campaign those who really tried to subvert the electoral process are being protected by the same political hacks running the phony investigations.[121],[122]

As Sperry reveals and relates:[123]

New revelations have surfaced that the Obama administration abused

---

[120] Sperry, P., *New York Post*, 5-26-17, accessed 6-18-19, https://nypost.com/2017/05/26/how-team-obama-tried-to-hack-the-election/

[121] Durben, T., *Zerohedge*, 5-25-17, Accessed 6-18-19, https://www.zerohedge.com/news/2017-05-25/unclassified-documents-show-obama-intel-agency-secretly-spied-americans-years

[122] *One News Page*, 5-25-17, accessed 6-18-19, https://www.onenewspage.com/n/Markets/75e8pyq8x/Unclassified-Documents-Show-Obama-Intel-Agency-Secretly-Spied.htm

[123] Sperry, P., *New York Post*, 5-26-17, accessed 6-18-19, https://nypost.com/2017/05/26/how-team-obama-tried-to-hack-the-election/

intelligence during the election by launching a massive domestic spy campaign that included snooping on Trump officials.

The irony is mind-boggling: Targeting political opposition is long a technique of police states like Russia, which Team Obama has loudly condemned for allegedly using its own intelligence agencies to hack into our election.

The revelations, as well as testimony this week from former Obama intel officials, show the extent to which the Obama administration politicized and weaponized intelligence against Americans.

We now know the National Security Agency under President Barack Obama routinely violated privacy protections while snooping through foreign intercepts involving US citizens — and failed to disclose the breaches, prompting the Foreign Intelligence Surveillance Court a month before the election to rebuke.

... The FISA court called it a "very serious Fourth Amendment issue" that NSA analysts — in violation of a 2011 rule change prohibiting officials from searching Americans' information without a warrant — "had been conducting such queries in violation of that prohibition, with much greater frequency than had been previously disclosed to the Court."

A number of those searches were made from the White House, and included private citizens working for the Trump campaign, some of whose identities were leaked to the media. The revelations earned a stern rebuke from the ACLU and from civil liberties champion Sen. Rand Paul.

We also learned this week that Obama intelligence officials really had no good reason attaching a summary of a dossier on Trump to a highly classified Russia briefing they gave to Obama just weeks before Trump took office.

Under congressional questioning Tuesday, Obama's CIA chief John Brennan said the dossier did not "in any way" factor into the agency's assessment that Russia interfered in the election. Why not? Because as Obama intel czar James Clapper earlier testified, "We could not corroborate the sourcing."[124]

But that didn't stop Brennan in January from attaching its contents to the official report for the president. He also included the unverified allegations in the briefing he gave Hill Democrats.

In so doing, Brennan virtually guaranteed that it would be leaked, which it promptly was.

In short, Brennan politicized raw intelligence. In fact, he politicized the entire CIA.

---

[124] Schultz, M. *New York Post*, 5-23-17, accessed 6-18-19 https://nypost.com/2017/05/23/ex-cia-chief-warned-of-russian-contact-with-trump-campaign-officials/

Langley vets say Brennan was the most politicized director in the agency's history. Former CIA field operations officer Gene Coyle said Brennan was "known as the greatest sycophant in the history of the CIA, and a supporter of Hillary Clinton before the election. I find it hard to put any real credence in anything that the man says."

Coyle noted that Brennan broke with his predecessors who stayed out of elections. Several weeks before the vote, he made it very clear he was pulling for Hillary. His deputy Mike Morell even came out and publicly endorsed her in the New York Times, claiming Trump was an "unwitting agent" of Moscow.

Brennan isn't just a Democrat. He's a radical leftist who in 1980 — during the height of the Cold War — voted for a Communist Party candidate for president.[125]

When Brennan rants about the dangers of strongman Vladimir Putin targeting our elections and subverting our democratic process, does he not catch at least a glimpse of his own reflection?

What he and the rest of the Obama gang did has inflicted more damage on the integrity of our electoral process than anything the Russians have done.

How does all this surveillance keep us safe? In Great Britain where there is more government surveillance than in any other western state it didn't help stop the recent Manchester bomber. According to press reports, he was known to the British intelligence services, he had traveled and possibly trained in bomb-making in Libya and Syria, his family members warned the authorities that he was dangerous, and he

[125] Kopan, T., CNN, 9-15-16, accessed 6-18-19 https://www.cnn.com/2016/09/15/politics/john-brennan-cia-communist-vote/

even flew terrorist flags over his house. What more did he need to do to signal that he may be a problem?[126]

Of course here in America our government's watchers are going to do it better ……. of course they will… ;--)

My question is: As they are watching us who watches them besides secret courts that report only to the perpetually re-elected guardians of the dysfunctional democratic process in a well-functioning oligarchy?

Never mind the facts. Don't pay any attention to who did what. Ignore an ex-president operating a deep state government in exile while orchestrating the Resist 45 Movement.

News Flash from

The ABCCBSNBCPBSCNNMSNBC Cartel:

---

[126] Paul, R., 5-29-17, *Newsmax*, accessed 6-18-19 https://www.newsmax.com/RonPaul/manchester-terrorism-surveillance-intelligence/2017/05/29/id/792913/

Drain the Swamp

THE RUSSIANS DID IT!!! THE RUSSIANS DID IT!!! THE RUSSIANS DID IT!!!

Drain the Swamp

Dispatch Nineteen

Resist 45 and the Government in Exile

Just when you thought it was safe to come out of the packed gun shows his extreme disjointed attacks on the Second Amendment inspired we're confronted with the sorry spectacle of a former American President speaking against us on foreign soil. I knew this guy reminded me of Jimmy Carter. When you hate America it doesn't matter what your job is or isn't you'll always find a venue that rejoices as you attack Old Glory.

After an all too brief (for us) vacation orchestrating the Resist 45 Movement from his lair in DC the Instigator-in-Chief couldn't resist a chance to visit the scene of one of his most famous speeches, Berlin. The fact that Europe's leading exponent of unlimited immigration German Chancellor Merkel agreed to receive him as a fellow head of state must have made his narcissistic head swim.

Here he is trying to upstage President Trump's well received visit to Saudi Arabia by attempting to push his shopworn platitudes down people's throats instead of playing golf with Tiger Woods. It seems no one told him Americans are tired of hearing the same old song no matter how loudly the supine Germans cheer as they're overwhelmed by the migration flood.

"We can't isolate ourselves," the former president said from a platform at the Brandenburg Gate. "We can't hide behind a wall." Of course everything should be taken in context. What was the Ex-President (oh how I love the 'Ex' part of that) saying: "One way we can do a better job is to create more opportunities for people in their home countries," Mr. Obama said. "If there are disruptions in these countries, if there is bad governance, if there is war, or if there is poverty in this new world we live in, we can't isolate ourselves — we can't hide behind a wall."[127]

And do you think that applies to everyone equally? According to the Washington Times, "Like so many liberals and 'progressives,' the former president does not mean that what he says should be taken literally, or even seriously. Walls, after all, are relative. America can't have one, but he can. The president lives in an enormous rented mansion behind a brick and stone wall built just for him, and which he has fitted out as the White House in exile, with a staff and lots of electronic communications gear, requiring the seizure of a quarter of a mile of a quiet residential street to be guarded by a Secret Service detail not much smaller than the platoon of heavily armed agents who kept him safe, sound and ready for action at 1600 Pennsylvania Avenue."

He even had some advice on child care, "A child on the other side of the border is no

---

[127] Pruden, W., *The Washington Post*, 5-25-17, accessed https://www.washingtontimes.com/news/2017/may/25/obama-attempts-government-in-exile/

less worthy of love and compassion than my own child. We can't distinguish between in terms of their worth and inherent dignity, and that they're deserving of shelter and love and education and opportunity."[128]

This from a man who Sen. Ron Johnson of Wisconsin, the chairman of the Senate Homeland Security Committee, just revealed directed Customs and Border Protection to release 16 members of the remarkably brutal MS-13 gang, freed to look at will for opportunities to kill and plunder.[129] "[The federal authorities] apprehended them, knew they were MS-13 gang members, and they processed them into our communities," the senator told his committee. How does this help provide safety for American children when these gang members terrorize our schools and communities?[130]

These globalists are more interested in advancing their agenda than in protecting America and its citizens.

---

[128] Ibid.
[129] Ibid.
[130] Ibid.

According to one of their minions, a senior judge on the far-left Ninth Circuit Court of Appeals, "Judges are humiliated and dehumanized whenever they must enforce the nation's immigration laws."[131] Judges are humiliated when they have to enforce laws? What kind of tin hat wearing alternate reality is this puffed-up self-anointed Carter appointed king in a black robe coming from? What set this ruler of men in a rage against the machine?

He was unable to block the orderly repatriation of an illegal immigrant who has two drunk driving convictions, plus a U.S. wife and three children. The outraged jurist complained, "We are unable to prevent [Andres] Magana Ortiz's removal, yet it is contrary to the values of this nation and its legal system."[132] In his blast from on high he continued, "We are compelled to deny Mr. Magana Ortiz's request for a stay of removal because we do not have the

---

[131] Munro, N., *Breitbart*, 6-5-17, accessed https://www.breitbart.com/politics/2017/06/05/dhs-officers-humiliate-judges-enforcing-immigration-laws-declares-judge/
[132] Ibid.

authority to grant it. We are not, however, compelled to find the government's action in this case fair or just. ... The government's decision to remove Magana Ortiz diminishes not only our country but our courts, which are supposedly dedicated to the pursuit of justice. Magana Ortiz and his family are in truth not the only victims. Among the others are judges who, forced to participate in such inhumane acts, suffer a loss of dignity and humanity as well. I concur as a judge, but as a citizen I do not."[133]

This judge is a perfect representative of the Deep State, the permanent government. They don't care who is elected or what the people may want. They have their agenda and they're going to continue to try and shove it down our throat until we either accept it or choke.

A president in exile leading a resistance movement against the man elected to succeed him, a Deep State of bureaucrats dedicated to the disruption of the government they are sworn to serve. What are we to do?

_____

[133] Ibid.

Drain the Swamp

Why worry when we can pray?

Keep the faith. Keep the peace. We shall
overcome.

Dispatch Twenty

IMPEACH TRUMP!!!!

That is the screech we're about to hear emanating from the denizens of the swamp. It is beginning to percolate already. Though predicted in this column by this author before the inauguration it still has a jarring impact on the senses.

Back in the Dream Times when the Deep State was able to turn Watergate into a silent coup the precedent was set. If someone tries to overturn the moneychanger's tables they must be destroyed. If it's a president, even one elected for the sole purpose of adding some reality to the mirage of a dysfunctional democracy portrayed by our functioning oligarchy, they must be hounded out of office, disgraced, and discredited.

That's the play book. The perpetually re-elected hacks aided and abetted by the ABCCBSNBCCNNMSNBCPBS Cartel and their paleo partners in print have latched on to their intended weapon, "The Russians are coming! The Russians are coming!"

No matter that the initial facts of the story are ludicrous: the fictional Golden Shower Dossier[134] and the Russian hack of the DNC, which was in fact an inside job.[135] It doesn't matter that the very foundation of the Russian collusion theory is built on sand; we now have a Special Counselor. We can't call him a Special Prosecutor because there is no legal foundation to appoint a Special Prosecutor, so if we call him a Special Counselor that should fool all of us out here in fly-over country.

Prosecutors always believe whoever they are investigating is guilty and that their job

[134] Gillespie, N., *reason*, 10-1-17, accessed 6-18-19 https://reason.com/2017/01/10/hey-heres-that-obviously-fake-dossier-cl
[135] *World Net Daily*, 5-15-19, accessed 6-18-19 https://www.wnd.com/2017/05/dead-dnc-staffer-had-contact-with-wikileaks/

is to find enough evidence to prove what they believe. Innocent until you are proven guilty, right. Anyone who has ever been lucky enough to have been involved in a criminal trial and lived to talk about it knows how that feels in reality. It inspired some to look at the courthouse and say, "It may say justice on the outside but there isn't any on the inside."

Remember the Valerie Plame investigation? Someone blew her cover as an undercover CIA operative. Before the investigation even started they knew who did it. Eventually after a few years and millions of dollars they never prosecuted anyone for the leak; instead they prosecuted Lewis "Scooter" Libby the Chief of Staff of Vice President Dick Chaney for inconsistencies in his testimony.[136]

These are search and destroy missions. They are looking to get at least one conviction to justify all of their expense and to puff up the reputations of the scalp

---

[136] Herman, A., *Commentary*, 6-2015, accessed https://www.commentarymagazine.com/articles/the-smearing-of-scooter-libby/

hunters who run them. This Special "Counselor" is one of the closest associates of James "The Leaker" Comey.[137] He is staffing his office with Obama and Hillary supporters and we're supposed to believe his investigation of a non-crime that never happened will produce objective results that anyone anywhere would imagine are justice?[138]

Witch hunts find witches. That's what they do. Have you ever been on a snipe hunt?[139] Ever find any snipes?

If anyone was interested in finding real collusion to disrupt an American election they could look into the subject of the DNC emails leaked to WikiLeaks; the proven collusion between the Hillary Clinton campaign, Donna Brazile, and Debbie

---

[137] Jarrett, G., Fox News, 6-12-19, accessed 6-18-19 https://www.foxnews.com/opinion/gregg-jarrett-are-mueller-and-comey-colluding-against-trump-by-acting-as-co-special-counsel
[138] Pavich, K., *Townhall*, 6-13-17, accessed https://townhall.com/tipsheet/katiepavlich/2017/06/13/hmmm-special-counsel-muellers-team-sure-is-stacked-with-democrat-donors-n2340655
[139] Urban Dictionary, accessed 6-18-19 https://www.urbandictionary.com/define.php?term=snipe%20hunt

Drain the Swamp

Wasserman Schultz. Did you ever notice that none of the principles ever denied what was in the leaked emails, they merely complained about who leaked what to who. Why isn't there a Special Counselor looking in to how these people stacked the cards against poor old Bernie Sanders? He said all along the election was rigged and he was right after all. Why no interest in this? It doesn't serve to keep the swamp damp that's why.

Our elite masters, the perpetually re-elected, the Deeps State, and the Media Cartel are setting the stage. They must drive Trump from office before he can actually drain the swamp. They must drive him out disgraced and repudiated or else we poor blind masses might figure out that we don't need technocrats to rule us.

I am for establishing a new political party. I think it should be the Telephone Book Party. I think we could pick the first 535 names out of any phone book in the country and get a Congress at least as good as the best one that money can buy. At least that way we might get some actual working people in there.

Until my new party figures out how to win a mandate we have to endure with what we have and these political savants are determined to undue the results of the last election. None of their fellow swamp dweller won, so they have banded together and the twin headed bird of prey that is the government party is clearly on display.

They won't let little things like votes, or facts, or what's good for America get in their way. No, they will soldier on and soon we will hear this predator's screech "IMPEACH TRUMP!!!! IMPEACH TRUMP!!!!" echoing through the land.

Dispatch Twenty-one

Did Illegals Voting Give Hillary the Edge?

The AntiFa Resist 45 Movement loves to point out that Hillary won the popular vote.

However, if you get down into the weeds a bit the picture that materializes isn't quite what we have been led to believe by the Democrat Party, their bully-boy street thugs, or their media megaphone.

If you take California out of the equation it is a completely different picture.[140]

> If you look at every other measure, Trump was the clear and decisive winner in this election.

---

[140] Vespa, M., *Townhall*, 12-17-16, accessed 6-18-19 https://townhall.com/tipsheet/mattvespa/2016/12/17/without-california-trump-would-won-14-million-more-votes-than-clinton-n2261014

Number of states won:
Trump: 30
Clinton: 20

Trump: +10

Number of electoral votes won:
Trump: 306
Clinton: 232

Trump: + 68

Ave. margin of victory in winning states:
Trump: 56%
Clinton: 53.5%

Trump: + 2.5 points

Popular vote total:
Trump: 62,958,211
Clinton: 65,818,318

Clinton: + 2.8 million

Popular vote total outside California:
Trump: 58,474,401
Clinton: 57,064,530

Trump: + 1.4 million

In other words, if you take California out of the popular vote equation, then Trump wins the rest of the country by 1.4 million votes. And if California voted like every other Democratic state — where Clinton averaged 53.5% wins — Clinton and Trump end up in a virtual popular vote tie. Then again for several reasons California doesn't vote like every other state. Besides the fact that it has become a one party State it isn't called Mexifornia for nothing. It is the destination of choice for more illegals coming north for economic and social reasons than any other State. Although we all know and have experienced the reality that in the aftermath of open borders illegals are now a sizable portion of the population anywhere you go in the U.S. of A.

Why does this have an impact on our understanding of the 2016 election?

Remember President Trump's famous tweet:

In addition to winning the Electoral College in a landslide, I won the popular vote if you deduct the millions of people who voted illegally

For this he was ridiculed by the ABCNBCCBSCNNMSNBCPBSNPR Cartel who presented it as nothing more than a "Twitter-born conspiracy theory." [141] Investor's Business Daily once again did the heavy lifting that the Lamestream Media refuses to do. In an editorial they provide us facts and projections based on actual studies, surveys, and scholarly research as opposed to the baseless character assassination which the media megaphone tries to pass off as journalism.

Such as a study in 2014 in the online Electoral Studies Journal which made a quite similar claim:[142] In the 2008 and 2010 elections, they said, as many as 2.8 million illegal noncitizen votes were cast, "enough

---

[141] Mack, E., Newsmax, 6-25-17, accessed 6-18-19 https://www.newsmax.com/Newsfront/non-citizens-may-be-voter-rolls/2017/06/25/id/798075/
[142] Science Direct, accessed 6-18-19 https://www.sciencedirect.com/science/article/pii/S0 261379414000973

to change meaningful election outcomes including Electoral College votes and congressional elections," said the study, authored by Jesse T. Richman and Gushan A. Chattha, both of Old Dominion University, and David C. Earnest of George Mason University. Which contained this bombshell: "Noncitizen votes likely gave Senate Democrats the pivotal 60th vote needed to overcome filibusters in order to pass health care reform and other Obama administration priorities in the 111th Congress."[143]

Concerning the possibility that as the President said illegals had an impact on the popular vote totals; a new study by Just Facts, a libertarian conservative think tank that used data from a large Harvard/You.Gov study that every two years samples tens of thousands of voters, including some who admit they are noncitizens and thus can't vote legally.

The findings are eye-opening. In 2008, as many as 5.7 million

---

[143] Ibid.

noncitizens voted in the election. In 2012, as many as 3.6 million voted, the study said.

In 2016, the U.S. Census Bureau estimates that there were 21.0 million adult noncitizens in the U.S., up from 19.4 million in 2008. It is therefore highly likely that millions of noncitizens cast votes in 2016.

And it was no accident. Democrats had extensive get-out-the-vote campaigns in areas heavily populated by illegal aliens. As far back as 2008, Obama made sure that those who wanted to vote knew it was safe, announcing that election records would not be cross-checked with immigration databases.

And last year, the Obama White House supported a court injunction that kept Kansas, Alabama and Georgia from requiring proof of citizenship to register to vote. The message was sent, loud and clear: If you're a noncitizen or here illegally, don't be afraid. You're free to vote. No one will stop you.

We don't know the exact number of illegal votes. No one does. But the data that are available suggest that the number of illegal votes was substantial — probably in the millions, as Trump said — and likely had a significant impact on the election's outcome.[144]

Think about this for a moment. To become an American Citizen a person has to pass a test on American History in English. These people would have no need for a ballot printed in another language. They can read English. That is a requirement of citizenship. In every State of our nation ballots are printed in Spanish. Since citizens have no need of them, who are they printed for? Isn't the answer self-evident?

---

[144] *Just Facts Daily*, 12-15-16, accessed 6-18-19 https://www.justfactsdaily.com/substantial-numbers-of-non-citizens-vote-illegally-in-u-s-elections/

Drain the Swamp

How can we avoid this type of fraud in the future?

First of all we could have fewer illegals in our country. Secondly we could require that people show proof of citizenship in order to register to vote. Also we could allow States to purge voter rolls of the dead, cross reference voter rolls across State lines, and require a photo ID to vote. Perhaps as the rule of law is re-instituted after the unconstitutional excesses of the Obamanation we will see such commonsense procedures instituted.

The truth will always eventually win out over the lie. And just as we can rest assured that those who believe the greatest lie of all time will eventually bow their knee and proclaim, "Jesus is Lord," so to we can rest assured that even in this fallen world the truth is always visible to those who seek it.

Did illegals voting in 2016 give Hillary the edge in the popular vote?

Sure they did.

Drain the Swamp

Dispatch Twenty-two

Exposing the ABCCBSNBCCNNMSNBCPBSNPR Cartel

Recent revelations by the last investigative reporter in America, James O'Keefe the founder of Project Veritas, expose the Corporations Once Known as the Mainstream Media; the ABCCBSNBCCNNMSNBCPBSNPR Cartel for what it is. A conglomeration of private and publicly sponsored corporations dedicated to leading us from America to Amerika.

When Project Veritas released a fourth secretly recorded video episode in its CNN series. In this episode, the presstitutes' worst nightmare of reality TV, a Project Veritas reporter spoke with CNN associate producer Jimmy Carr who according to his LinkedIn page has been with CNN since 2013 as a production assistant and associate producer. In the video Carr doesn't appear to know he's being recorded. The Veritas reporter asks if it "would be fair to question the intellect of the American voter."[145]

"Oh, no. They're stupid as s---," replied the CNN "New Day" associate producer.

Carr continued, "On the inside, we all recognize he is a clown, that he is hilariously unqualified for this, he's really bad at this, and that he does not have America's best interests."[146]

"We recognize he's just f---ing crazy."[147]

"Here's the deal: This is a man who's not actually a Republican,"[148] Carr added. "He just adopted that because that was the party he thought he could win in. He doesn't believe anything that these people believe."[149]

---

[145] Concha, J., *The Hill*, 6-30-17, accessed 6-18-19 https://thehill.com/homenews/media/340210-cnn-producer-on-new-okeefe-video-voters-are-stupid-crazy
[146] Ibid.
[147] Ibid.
[148] Ibid.
[149] Ibid.

"Ninety percent of us are on board with just the fact that he's crazy,"[150] he added.

Project Veritas also released a video of a medical producer at CNN saying that while he believes the Trump-Russia narrative is "bulls---,"[151] CEO Jeff Zucker has instructed his employees to focus on it to help boost the network's ratings.

According to Washington Free Beacon, in the video, CNN producer John Bonifield said the network's focus on potential ties between President Donald Trump's campaign and Russia is based on ratings. The pull quotes are amazing.

"I mean, it's mostly bullshit right now. Like, we don't have any big giant proof,"[152] Bonifield said of the Russia story. It is unclear when he made the statement.

"And so I think the president is right to say, like, 'Look, you are witch-hunting me. You

---

[150] Ibid.
[151] Crookston, P., *The Washington Free Beacon*, 6-27-17, accessed 6-19-19
https://freebeacon.com/politics/project-veritas-cnn-producer-russia-reporting-mostly-bull-st/
[152] Ibid.

have no smoking gun. You have no real proof,'"[153] Bonifield said.

Once again according to Washington Free Beacon, Bonfield explained that ratings motivate CNN's focus on the Russia story. Asked why the network aired so much Russia coverage, Bonifield said, "It's ratings."[154]

"Our ratings are incredible right now," he added.

Bonifield also said that the emphasis on Russia came from upper management. He detailed a meeting in which President Jeff Zucker advised staff to focus on the Paris climate accord for a day and a half before returning to Russia.[155]

"The CEO of CNN said in our internal meeting, he said, 'Good job everybody covering the climate accords, but we're done with it. Let's get back to Russia,'"[156] Bonifield said.

---

[153] Ibid.
[154] Ibid.
[155] Idid.
[156] Ibid.

Bonifield described a jaded business culture at CNN and in cable news generally.[157]

"All the nice cutesy little ethics that used to get talked about in journalism school, you're just like, 'That's adorable, that's adorable. This is a business,'"[158] he said.

"They gotta do what they gotta do to make their money,"[159] Bonifield added. "And so I love the news business, but I am very cynical about it. At the same time, so are most of my colleagues."[160]

Bonifield said that CNN would have turned off its liberal viewers if the network strongly scrutinized former President Barack Obama, but Trump is "good for business."[161]

In Part Two of the current series of O'Keefe videos Van Jones the professional leftist and former Obama Administration official is stopped on the street and filmed. Here is

---

[157] Ibid.
[158] Ibid.
[159] Ibid.
[160] Ibid.
[161] Ibid.

how the conversation between the Project Veritas journalist and Jones progressed:[162]

PV Journalist: "Hey man, we met in Palm Springs a few years back."

Van Jones: "Hey good to see you man, you good?"

PV Journalist: "What do you think is going to happen this week with the whole Russia thing?"

Van Jones: "The Russia thing is just a big nothing burger."

PV Journalist: "Really?"

Van Jones: "Yeah."

So what does all this fake news and political propaganda add up to?

We now have a Special Counselor investigating obstruction of justice when there was no underlying crime to begin with. How can that fail to bring justice for

---

[162] YouTube,
https://www.youtube.com/watch?v=I2G360HrSAs

the American people? My prediction: They will convict someone of something.

We all know that there were people working day and night to corrupt our electoral process in 2016. It was Clinton and the DNC Ratpack out to stack the deck against socialist Bernie Sanders. And there was obstruction of justice too in the deleting of email evidence.

However the truth doesn't fit the playbook of the left. They're determined to reverse the results of the 2016 election because they didn't win.

The presstitutes tell us that O'Keefe is not to be believed. That he is disreputable and underhanded. A tactic right out of their guru Saul Alinsky, attack the messenger. They can't deny what they've said because we can see and hear them as they speak. So just like the hacked emails they want us to look at how the information was gathered so we won't realize the information exposes them for what they are, the media megaphone for the Democrat Party, the ABCCBSNBCCNNMSNBCPBSNPR Cartel.

Dispatch Twenty-three

Today it's Eurasia Tomorrow it's Eastasia

If you've never read George Orwell's 1984 you might miss this reference. It exposes the unreal reality show that's called foreign relations by some and "The Great Game"[163] by those who play it. The USSR was Hitler's mortal enemy until he signed a non-aggression pact which lasted until he invaded.

Today the show must go on and for the show to go on there must be a villain. Enter the "NEW" Hitler.

The Media Cartel constantly pushes Russia forward as our enemy and their leader Vladimir Putin as the new Hitler. We are told he constantly attacks freedom

---

[163] GlobalSecurity.org, accessed 6-19-19
https://www.globalsecurity.org/military/world/war/great-game.htm

wherever it is found and that he is trying to re-create that failed socialist nightmare, the USSR.

What Putin says as opposed to what we're told he says:[164]

From his annual Christmas press conference in 2016 here are some excerpts of what our modern day Hitler had to say.

In a nearly four-hour question and answer session, the Russian president held forth on the state of his country and the world, saying that there is an international push for a New World Order that will *"remove national sovereignty"* and *"destroy identity and of God-created diversity."*

To reach this goal, Putin states that Western elites have begun rejecting the roots that their society was built on.

"Many Western states have taken the way where they deny or reject their own roots, including their Christian roots which form

---

[164] *The Guardian*, 12-23-16, accessed 6-19-19 https://www.theguardian.com/world/live/2016/dec/23/vladimir-putins-annual-press-conference-live-updates

the basis of Western civilization. In these countries, the moral basis and any traditional identity are being denied – national, religious, cultural and even gender identities are being denied or relativized."

"In these countries, the moral basis and any traditional identity are being denied – national, religious, cultural and even gender identities are being denied or relativized. There, politics treats a family with many children as equal to a homosexual partnership (juridically).

The excesses and exaggerations of political correctness in these countries indeed leads to serious consideration for the legitimization of parties that promote the propaganda of pedophilia.

"The people in many European states are actually ashamed of their religious affiliations and are indeed frightened to speak about them."

Putin says that the situation has become so extreme in Western culture, that people are now taught that "*Faith in God is equal to faith in Satan*". To say otherwise would be to risk being politically incorrect — the great crime of our age.

"Christian holidays and celebrations are abolished or 'neutrally' renamed, as if one were ashamed of those Christian holidays. With this method one hides away the deeper moral values of these celebrations.

"And these countries try to force this model onto other countries, globally. I am deeply convinced that this is a direct way to the degradation and primitivization of culture. This leads to deeper demographic and moral crisis in the West. What can be a better evidence for the moral crisis of a human society (in the West) than the loss of its reproductive function?"

"Today nearly all 'developed' Western countries cannot survive reproductively, not even with the help of migrants.

Without the moral values that are rooted in Christianity and other world religions, without rules and moral values which have formed and been developed over millennia, people will inevitably lose their human dignity."

Putin was unapologetic about Russia's determination to defend Western values.

"And we think it is right and natural to defend and preserve these moral (Christian) values."

"At the same time as this process at a national level in the West, we observe on an international level the attempts to create a unipolar, unified model of the world, to relativize and remove institutions of international right and national sovereignty.

"In such a unified, unipolar world there is no place for sovereign states. Such a world needs merely vassals.

"From a historical perspective, such a unipolar world would mean the surrender of one's own identity and of God-created diversity."

Does that sound like Hitler to you? If it does perhaps you should re-read Mein Kampf because it doesn't quite read the same to me. Many of these are the same comments made by conservatives in America. The multicultural politically correct progressives are leading the West down the primrose path to cultural destruction.

Instead of the moral fiber to stand up for and defend Western values and civilization we are offered the corrupt substitute of the Neocons, war. We may have the most powerful armies and the most destructive weapons. But are they being used to defend who we are. Or are they being used to feather the nests of oligarchs and plutocrats who live in gated communities and will never be impacted by the mess they are making?

The Political/Military/Industrial/Media Complex always needs an enemy. They must have a villain if they are to sell there shopworn tales to the gullible. Today it's Eurasia. Tomorrow it's Eastasia. Yesterday it was Saddam. Today it's Putin.

Supporting what America stands for does not necessarily translate into blindly supporting who stands for America.

This is not an article promoting Vladimir Putin as anything besides what he is, the nationalistic leader of Russia. It is an article pointing out that in many ways we are being sold a bill of goods.

There is turmoil in the Ukraine and Crimea has rejoined Russia not because the new Hitler invaded but because of American instigation of a coup against a democratically elected president and the installation of a handpicked replacement. It is America and not Russia that is acting contrary to the accepted laws of the UN in Syria.[165] Russia is the ally of the UN recognized government. The USA operates in contravention of the UN rules of engagement.[166]

The Neocons and their army of Deep State Bureaucrats continue to plot, propagandize, and manipulate no matter who is in power.

---

[165] Milne, S. *The Guardian*, 4-30-14, accessed 6-19-19
https://www.theguardian.com/commentisfree/2014/apr/30/russia-ukraine-war-kiev-conflict
[166] Doebler, C., *Counter Punch*, 4-7-17, accessed 6-19-19
https://www.counterpunch.org/2017/04/07/why-the-united-states-use-of-force-against-syria-violates-international-law/

Drain the Swamp

We don't need to be the straw man or the cat's paw for any backroom gang of ideologues. What we need is what we voted for, "America First!' and "Make America Great Again!" Let's not get sidetracked into a war with Russia, China, Iran, or Bolivia.

We need our president doing what he does best inspiring Middle America. I am fan of inspirational words and The Donald knows how to ring my bell. In his speech to the Polish people he said, "The West became great not because of paperwork and regulations but because people were allowed to chase their dreams and pursue their destinies."

Hopefully our president will see through all the blah-blah-blah in the Media, in Congress, and among the Deep State Government Party hacks. Keep the peace and allow us the freedom to chase our dreams and pursue our destinies.

Drain the Swamp

Dispatch Twenty-four

When Your Strategy Doesn't Work
Check Your Tactics

The Republican House voted more than fifty times to repeal Obummercare. Even the Republican Senate did the same thing a few times while the Progressives' Obamassiah was running the State and not just the Deep State. Now that the Republicans have the whole shooting match they can't seem to hit the target.

Maybe it's the strategy of doing it all in one BIG omnibus bill filled with payoffs, bribes, and meant to restructure the entire healthcare industry in one fell swoop that is causing the problem. I know, I know the perpetually re-elected love their omnibus mega-bills just because they can shoehorn in massive payoffs and bribes without anyone being the wiser, but this just isn't working.

Besides if the vote in November was for anything it was for ending business as usual. It was for reining in the two-headed Republicrat bird of prey. It was for righting the Ship of State before it crashes on the reef of bankruptcy. It was for taking control of our Republic from the technocrats and the professional socialist redistributionist hustlers and returning it to the hands of those who work to make America great, again.

Obviously from the on-going "There's a Russian Under Every Bush" reality show in Congress the inmates are still running the asylum in the capital of the world. The Republican variety of Progressives after all their valiant efforts to repeal Obummercare when there was no chance it would actually repeal Obummercare don't really want to remove the governments talons from one sixth of our economy.

An axiom of socialist logic is that once an entitlement is enacted it can never be repealed because the people become strung-out on the idea that someone owes them something. Have you ever tried taking candy from a baby or a bone from a dog? It adds up to about the same thing as trying to convince people addicted to free stuff that they don't need the free stuff.

We have a President who wants to fulfill his campaign promises. He wants to repeal Obummercare and replace it with sensible free market solutions, he wants to lower taxes for working people and small businesses, he wants to allow Corporations to re-patriate the hundreds of billions locked up overseas because of confiscatory taxes at home, and he wants to build the wall. He wants to do all these things, and if he was able to do them we would once again have a health care system that is dynamic, cutting edge and providing the best care for the most people, the economy would take off like a rocket, and with the tide of migration stopped those who are here would have the breathing space to assimilate and become Americans. If he could accomplish these things he would be a shoe-in for re-election and end up as one of the most successful presidents in History. This is exactly why the best

Congress money can buy will never pass any of these things.

Instead the plutocrats of the Potomac are playing legislative games. They are using their Omnibus hand-jive to mask the fact that their repeal doesn't really repeal very much. They want to keep the taxes, keep the mandates, and keep the subsidies. They want to bail out the insurance companies, payoff their donors, and pad the bill with bribes for every lobbyist and special interest group with enough clout to get skin in the game.

Luckily we have some watchmen on the walls who are using every megaphone they can find to warn us about the sow's ear being passed off as a silk purse. Senators like Rand Paul and Mike Lee are leading the fight. Congressmen like Dave Brat are speaking truth to power and shining a light in the darkness.

If the Republicans were really serious about repeal and replace they wouldn't use the omnibus absurdity, but they would instead deal with this in bite size chunks. Repeal Obummercare and return the country to the status quo ante. Then pass individual bills to make the changes they want to see. For instance one bill to provide pre-existing condition coverage, another to allow insurance companies to sell across state lines, another for tort reform, another to streamline the FDA, etc.

All these bills could be just a few pages long written in Standard English instead of the hundreds and thousands of pages of insurance speak that clutter the omnibus monstrosities.

In other words, when your strategy doesn't work check your tactics. If the Mitch, Paul, and the GOP Pretenders were serious about fulfilling the campaign promises they made they would give us a hundred little victories instead of one major defeat. But if they did that President Trump would succeed. And if President Trump succeeds he points out the fact that we don't need these professional politicians to run our world. We can run it just fine ourselves.

Drain the Swamp

Dispatch Twenty-five

Hacked Emails Expose Hacks

The sore loser cry babies who refuse to accept the results of American voters will do anything to make the vote of the people for Donald Trump appear illegitimate. Their lame attempts at frivolous recounts only exposed their own corruption[167] and added votes to the Donald's bottom line. So it is time for a new approach.[168] Blame it on the Russians.

I remember back in the 1980s when we finally had a president with a plan to end the Cold War. These same bleeding heart

---

[167] Fox News Insider, 12-14-1`6, accessed 6-19-19 https://insider.foxnews.com/2016/12/14/steins-recount-turns-more-votes-voters-detroit
[168] Finnigahe Los Angeles Times, 12-12-16, accessed 6-19-19
https://www.latimes.com/nation/politics/trailguide/la-na-trailguide-updates-final-wisconsin-recount-tally-1481584948-htmlstory.html

limousine liberals fell all over themselves opposing the Gipper. They marched, they colluded with the enemy and they endlessly attacked him and his plan through their operatives masquerading as journalists in the Corporations Once Known as the Mainstream Media.[169]

Now when the evidence is flimsy at best and manufactured at worst they are indignantly riding their high horses to another catastrophic defeat. Even the help of all the RINOs in Congress won't help these repudiated Clintonistas put Humpty Dumpty Hillary back together again.

Their megaphones in the media are filling the airwaves with the lie that all our intelligence services agree the Russians hacked our election and caused the defeat of the anointed and the victory of the barbarians.[170]

---

[169] Radosh, R., *The Daily Beast*, 1-29-17, accessed 6-19-19 https://www.thedailybeast.com/when-the-left-longed-for-russian-political-interference

[170] Sivak, D., *The Daily Caller*, 6-1-17, accessed 6-19-18 https://dailycaller.com/2017/06/01/fact-check-did-17-intel-agencies-all-agree-russia-hacked-the-dnc-podesta/

Let's see how that squares with reality.

Top US Spy Agency Doesn't Back CIA View on Russia Hacking

According to Reuters the leaders of the U.S. intelligence community do not embrace a CIA assessment that Russian cyber-attacks were aimed at helping Republican President-elect Donald Trump win the 2016 election.[171] While the Office of the Director of National Intelligence (ODNI) does not dispute the CIA's analysis of Russian hacking operations, it does not endorse their assessment because there is a lack of conclusive evidence that Moscow intended to boost Trump over Democratic opponent Hillary Clinton.

The position of the Office of the Director of National Intelligence (ODNI), which oversees the seventeen agency-strong U.S. intelligence communities, gives Trump an informed position to dispute the CIA assessment.

---

[171] *Newsmax*, 12-13-16, accessed 6-19-19 https://www.newsmax.com/Newsfront/russia-hack-director-national-intelligence/2016/12/13/id/763661/

Former Army Intel Officer Rejects Hack Theory: CIA's Brennan Playing 'Info Warfare'

A retired Army intelligence officer dismissed the theory that the Russians hacked the election in favor of Donald Trump, instead putting forth his own theory — CIA Director John Brennan is playing political games.[172]

Retired Lt. Col. Tony Shaffer stated that in his opinion Brennan is trying to undermine the president-elect out of deference to his old boss, President Barack Obama.

Shaffer said, "This is purely political, and I believe that John Brennan is a political animal. Everything they are telling me is Brennan is doing this out of loyalty to Ex-President Obama. It's called information operations, information warfare, and that's what I believe is going on."[173]

Ultimately what's more dangerous the DNC hack or the criminality it exposed?

---

[172] Swanson, M., *Newsmax*, 12-13-19, accessed 6-19-19 https://www.newsmax.com/Newsfront/Russia-Election-Hacking-CIA/2016/12/13/id/763648/
[173] Ibid.

These leaked emails, whether released by Russia, China, or some teenager in his mother's basement expose possible criminal activity by Secretary Clinton and New York's Sixth Crime Family using her office as the launching pad for a pay-to-play scam to solicit tens of millions of dollars from foreign heads of state.[174]

There was also evidence that Clinton's campaign staff colluded with their not-so-covert supporters over at the Clinton News Network (CNN) before one of her debates with the Donald in order to help her in the debate and sway the results of the election.[175] As a matter of fact though they still deny it happened Donna Brazile has admitted that she shared the questions with Hillary before the debate.[176] If that isn't cheating and colluding to influence the vote I don't know what is.

---

[174] Kerik, B., *Newsmax*, 12-13-19, accessed 6-19-19 https://www.newsmax.com/Newsfront/Bernard-Kerik-DNC-Hack-Criminality/2016/12/13/id/763678/
[175] Ibid.
[176] Scarry, E., *The Washington Examiner*, 3-17-17, accessed 6-19-19 https://www.washingtonexaminer.com/donna-brazile-finally-admits-she-shared-debate-questions-with-clinton-campaign

In addition,[177] Clinton's campaign staff and the DNC colluded to undermine the presidential campaign of Bernie Sanders. This is what the hacked emails from the DNC reveal never mind who leaked them the truth is the truth.

Clinton's staff and members of the DNC all knew that Sanders was soliciting millions of dollars for his presidential campaign. All the while they also knew that while he was doing so, they were conspiring to do everything in their power to undermine his campaign and guarantee his failure. According to some lawyers, that could be seen as honest services fraud.[178]

Then there is the history of American politicians working with the Russians to influence our elections. Hint: it wasn't conservatives and it wasn't Putin.

---

[177] Kerik, B., *Newsmax*, 12-13-16, accessed 6-19-19 https://www.newsmax.com/Newsfront/Bernard-Kerik-DNC-Hack-Criminality/2016/12/13/id/763678/
[178] Ibid.

Drain the Swamp

In an article by Michael Reagan in Newsmax: [179]

Democrats Secretly Worked With Russia to Oppose My Dad

Former intelligence officer Herbert Romerstein dug through the Soviet archives after the fall of the USSR and uncovered secret documents written by KGB agent Victor Chebrikov. The documents revealed that Senator Edward "Ted" Kennedy had sent a friend, former Senator John Tunney of California, to contact the KGB. Tunney's mission: undermine then-President Jimmy Carter.

On March 5, 1980, as Kennedy was challenging Carter in the primaries, Tunney met with the KGB and urged the Soviets to sabotage Carter's foreign policy efforts. It's amazing: Two high-ranking Democrats — a sitting U.S. senator and a former senator — sought Soviet help in undermining American

---

[179] Reagan, M., *Newsmax*, 12-13-16, accessed 6-19-19
https://www.newsmax.com/MichaelReagan/democrats-russia-ronald-reagan/2016/12/13/id/763730/

foreign policy and manipulating an American election.

One 1980 document stated that Kennedy offered to condemn President Carter's policy toward the Soviet occupation of Afghanistan in exchange for KGB help. News accounts of that period prove that Kennedy did, in fact, openly criticize Carter's Afghanistan policy.

Even more amazing: President Carter himself was also willing to jump into bed with the Soviets. In the closing days of the 1980 presidential campaign, while trailing Ronald Reagan in the polls, Jimmy Carter sent a political ally, industrialist Armand Hammer, to a secret meeting with Soviet ambassador Anatoly Dobrynin at the embassy in Washington. Hammer asked the Soviets to help Carter win votes in key states by allowing Jewish "refuseniks" to emigrate to Israel. The Soviets rejected Hammer's request.

In January 1984, former President Carter approached Ambassador Dobrynin in person. Carter wanted to derail President Reagan's defense buildup, and asked for help from the Evil Empire in unseating

President Reagan. It's not clear if the Soviets gave Carter what he wanted.

Then there's Speaker of the House Thomas P. "Tip" O'Neill. He privately told Ambassador Dobrynin that it was in everyone's best interests if the Soviets would help the Democrats keep "that demagogue Reagan" from being re-elected. O'Neill warned Dobrynin that the "primitive instincts" of this "dangerous man" would plunge the world into war.

It must have amazed Anatoly Dobrynin that these prominent liberals — Ted Kennedy, Armand Hammer, Jimmy Carter, and Tip O'Neill — all viewed President Reagan as more dangerous than any Communist dictator. Historian Paul Kengor observed that the Soviet archives showed "the lengths to which some on the political left . . .were willing to go to stop Ronald Reagan."

Why did the KGB documents come to light? They surfaced because Ronald Reagan toppled the Evil Empire, ended the Cold War, and thwarted the joint Democrat-Soviet effort to manipulate the election.

And if all else fails we could always go to the horse's mouth. According[180] to Fortune magazine, "Julian Assange claims Russia isn't behind WikiLeaks' hacked Clinton emails."

The latest revelation in this unraveling story of Russian leaks and possible interference in the election of Donald Trump involves an explosive revelation[181] which will no doubt be hidden from the low-information voters who receive all their news from the ABCCBSNBCCNNMSNBC CABAL.

An ex-British ambassador who is now a WikiLeaks operative claims Russia did NOT provide Clinton emails - they were handed over to him at a D.C. park by an intermediary for 'disgusted' Democratic whistleblowers. Craig Murray, former British ambassador to Uzbekistan and a

---

[180] *Fortune*, 11-3-16, accessed 6-19-19 http://fortune.com/2016/11/03/julian-assange-wikileaks-russia-podesta-emails/
[181] Goodman, A., *The Daily Mail*, 12-14-16, accessed 6-19-19 https://www.dailymail.co.uk/news/article-4034038/Ex-British-ambassador-WikiLeaks-operative-claims-Russia-did-NOT-provide-Clinton-emails-handed-D-C-park-intermediary-disgusted-Democratic-insiders.html

close associate of WikiLeaks founder Julian Assange, told Dailymail.com that he flew to Washington, D.C. for a clandestine hand-off with one of the email sources in September.

Murray insisted that the DNC and Podesta emails published by WikiLeaks did not come from the Russians, and were given to the whistle-blowing group by Americans who had authorized access to the information.

Murray said, "Neither of [the leaks] came from the Russians. The source had legal access to the information. The documents came from inside leaks, not hacks."[182]

He said "The leakers were motivated by disgust at the corruption of the Clinton Foundation and the tilting of the primary election playing field against Bernie Sanders."[183]

Here's another bombshell exploding on the flank of the politically motivated fake news campaign by the Progressive establishment to de-legitimize the election of Donald

---

[182] Ibid.
[183] Ibid.

Trump. According to Frank Gaffney in Newsmax:[184]

In telephone conversations with Donald Trump, Ex-FBI Director (and self-admitted leaker) James Comey assured the president-elect there was no credible evidence that Russia influenced the outcome of the recent U.S. presidential election by hacking the Democratic National Committee and the emails of John Podesta, the chairman of Hillary Clinton's presidential campaign.

What's more, Comey told Trump that James Clapper, the director of National Intelligence, agreed with this FBI assessment.

The only member of the U.S. intelligence community who was ready to assert that the Russians sanctioned the hacking was John Brennan, the ex-director of the CIA, according to sources who were briefed on Comey's conversations with Trump.

---

[184] Kline, E., *Newsmax*, 12-16-16, accessed https://www.newsmax.com/Newsfront/comey-fbi-russia-trump/2016/12/14/id/764008/

"And Brennan takes his marching orders from President Obama," the sources quoted Comey as saying.

In Comey's view, the leaks to the New York Times and the Washington Post alleging that the Russians tried—and perhaps even succeeded—in tilting the election to Trump were a Democratic Party effort to delegitimize Trump's victory.

Looking at the leaks about this whole affair former House Intelligence Committee Chairman Pete Hoekstra told Newsmax TV, "It is not the agency that is doing this. It is rogue employees within the CIA who are leaking this information."[185]

Here's the real hack that attempted to subvert our election:[186]

---

[185] Beamon, T., *Newsmax*, 12-14-16, accessed 6 19 19 https://www.newsmax.com/Newsmax-Tv/CIA-Pete-Hoekstra-hacks-intelligence/2016/12/14/id/764026/
[186] *Detroit News*, 12-12-16, accessed 6-19-19 https://www.detroitnews.com/story/news/politics/2016/12/12/records-many-votes-detroits-precincts/95363314/

The recent re-count in Michigan revealed there were too many votes in 37% of Detroit's precincts

Detailed reports from the office of Wayne County Clerk Cathy Garrett show optical scanners at 248 of the city's 662 precincts, or 37 percent, tabulated more ballots than the number of voters tallied by workers in the poll books.

This is the same old same old vote rigging by the Democrat machines that have presided over the destruction of our great cities. What these political hacks have done to Detroit is what they were planning for the country as a whole. In other words; the hacked emails and the frivolous re-counts exposed the Hacks. And though they did their best to steal the election and today they are fighting to keep the truth hidden,[187] the working people of America finally got up off the couch, the silent majority final spoke with one voice, and instead of the managed decline of the

---

[187] Berger, J., Fox News, 67-30-17, accessed 6-19-19 https://www.foxnews.com/politics/dem-state-officials-refusing-to-cooperate-with-trump-voter-fraud-probe

Drain the Swamp

Obama-Clinton CABAL we are on the road to Make America Great Again!

Drain the Swamp

Dispatch Twenty-six

Lock Her Up

In America today most people choose their favorite brand of the ABCCBSNBCCNNMSNBCPBSNPR Cartel based on the charisma of the news reader, and don't waste their time tuning into other news options.

What are the criteria for their choice of a news outlet? Does the news reader look or sound authoritative? Are they better looking? Do they have a more pleasing voice? Are they a Male? Are they a female? Are they Gay? Are we not sure? Whatever the reason, it isn't because they say anything different. It often sounds like they all have the same writers and story selectors. The content is no different.

Do you want to hear the story about how the Republican Elite is trying to figure out some way to dump Trump before or after you hear the story about how The Donald is not fit for the highest office in the land or after? Do you want to learn about the latest polls that show everyone hates Trump before or after you hear how Trump the Traitor colluded with the Russians before or after you hear about the insane proposals of the racist homophobe misogynist Trump? Perhaps the line-up of the stories is slightly changed from one news clone to another but that's about it.

When I have a chance encounter and what passes for conversation with so many Kool-Aid drinking low information voters i.e progressive induhviduals the conversation usually goes like this:

Me: What do you think about _____ (fill in the blank)?

Progressive Induhvidual: Repeat what ABC, CBS, NBC, CNN, MSNBC, PBS, NPR, the New York Times, the Washington Post, USA Today, the Chicago Tribune, etc. has said recently stated as if this was their independently arrived at personal opinion.

Or if they are a Conservative Induhvidual: Repeat what Fox, the Wall Street Journal, the Weekly Standard, National Review, etc. has recently said.

It's almost impossible to find anyone who has actually read any books on topics of importance such as economics, politics, sociology, or the History that ties them all together.

Several times a year I attend meetings that are filled with nothing but PhDs, professors, and university administrators. All content experts in these very subjects as well as many others. The results are basically the same. The death of critical thinking has led to a deafening silence in the area of actual personal opinion, a dearth of dialogue, and a collapse of conversation. The American people, who at the time of the Founding saw blacksmiths discussing with candle makers the pros and cons of constitutions and the meaning of liberty or carpenters debating with plumbers the need for a free economy versus the need for public works. Just read the Federalist and the Anti-Federalist Papers, look at the level of thought and speech and ask yourself, "How do the public debate, and newspaper articles of contemporary America match up?" Today the public debate takes place at about a 3rd grade level compared to the graduate school of those earlier days.

What happened? Back then there weren't public schools. Churches and families educated their own. Today after generations of highly funded and severely structured public education we've successfully dumbed ourselves down to the lowest common denominator.

Look at the late great Bernie Sanders revolt which was contained by the elite in the Democrat Party and the Trump Revolution which overwhelmed the elite in the Republican Party it's obvious that we tax paying entities who inhabit flyover country whether of the right or left have had enough of the bi-coastal elite that's driving us over the cliff into the third world. Since their empty pantsuit blew the election and she can't carry the water for the donor class all the way to the bank obviously the elite controlled media has dropped their camouflage of objectivity and is all in to make sure Trump is destroyed.

At least there was one pseudo surprise in the Hollywood scripted replay of Primary Colors the Distaff Edition. After all of the frothing at the mouth Bernie supporters did. After they were so brave that they booed or turned their backs at the Democrat Party Spectacle in Philadelphia on their anointed queen. Low and behold their fearless leader fell into line and surprise surprise supported the mistress of manipulation. Then just as evidence surfaced that yes, the entire primary exercise was rigged from the beginning the mind-numb robots of the left who chanted and cheered for Bernie stood in line to cast their rationally considered and highly principled vote for the very person who engineered the fix, takes her money and marching orders from the crony capitalists, and is arguably the most corrupt person to ever run for the presidency. After the election, Bernie, the man of the people bought his third house[188] and settled in a

---

[188] Nguyen, T., *Vanity Fair*, 8-9-16, accessed 6-19-19

well feathered bed until next time he's needed to attack his fellow millionaires and billionaires.[189]

Who could have seen this coming except a blind man in a dark room with no media access?

The pre-programmed electorate combined with the usual fraud, imported voters and all the dead[190] people[191] who never leave[192] the voting rolls of the corrupt Democrat City fiefdoms, marched in lockstep to the polls to hand America lock-stock-and-barrel to the Clinton Crime Family.[193]

---

https://www.vanityfair.com/news/2016/08/bernie-sanders-summer-house

[189] Schwab, N., *Daily Mail*, 6-5-17, accessed 6-19-19 https://www.dailymail.co.uk/news/article-4574760/Socialism-rewarding-s-Bernie-millionaire.html

[190] Goldstein, D., CBS, 5-23-16

[191] Ballotpedia, accessed 6-19-19 https://ballotpedia.org/Dead_people_voting

[192] *World Net Daily*, 5-24-16, accessed 6-19-19 https://www.wnd.com/2016/05/hundreds-of-dead-voters-cast-ballots-decades-after-dying/

[193] Murdock, D., *National Review*, 5-27-16, accessed 6-19-19 https://www.nationalreview.com/2016/05/hillary-

However the November Miracle happened and instead of the Sleazy Don following the totally corrupt Donna back into the White House the Donald won.

Enough people swallowed the red pill and were willing to at least take a shot at shaking things up before we're swept away by the unregulated immigration invasion and state sponsored outsourcing that low and behold we didn't end up with another perpetually re-elected hack.

An old saying goes, "There are only two things that are certain in this life, death and taxes." We've all been programmed to accept this as an inevitable truism. Death to be sure is natural and inevitable. If you were born you'll die. Taxes however aren't a natural thing. They're in actuality the forced expropriation of funds from the productive taken through the use of the state's monopoly on the use of coercive force. And so, though they aren't natural and they aren't inevitable like death or gravity they may in realistic terms given the

---

clinton-bill-clinton-crime-family-where-politics-and-mafia-meet/

overwhelming preponderance of government power be unavoidable.

Our country refused to follow the dictates of the elite controlled media. America refused to become the turf of the Sleazy Donna from Chappaqua whose word parsing motto should be the Bart Simpson anthem, "I didn't do it! Nobody saw me do it! You can't prove anything." We chose not to let the White House once again become Bill's love nest. We refused to let the George Soros puppet in heels moves into the Oval Office with her rolodex of contributors both foreign and domestic.

So what do we have now? The Cartel and the politicians that follow them around like a children's pull toy on a string are screeching day and night the Russians! The Russians! They have Comey's BFF installed as the Special Counsel because of Comey's leaks. The stage is set for a sequel to the Progressives favorite thriller, "The Witch Hunt of Watergate."

Ding Dong the Witch is politically dead! But is this like when a queen dies? The Witch is politically dead long live the witch. Waiting in the wings is everyone's favorite Caucasian Indian from Massachusetts.

What's a freedom loving constitutionalist to do? How about every time the Progressives issue a subpoena for one of the President's followers we issue one for a Debbie Wasserman Schultz, or her Pakistani IT money launderer, or Bill Clinton, or Loretta Lynch, or any of the shady characters who actually tried to fix the election. How about a Special Counsel to investigate all the scandals of the Obummer nightmare, Fast and Furious, Benghazi, Lois Lerner and the IRS, or the serial unmasking of American citizens for political purposes? How about, "Lock her up!"

Why should we just roll over and take it? Why not take it and roll on instead? We won let's act like it!

Maybe I'm speaking out of turn or maybe I should remember the ever[194] growing[195]

---

[194] Alexander, R., *Townhall*, 8-9-16, accessed 6-19-19
https://townhall.com/columnists/rachelalexander/2016/08/09/clinton-body-count-or-leftwing-conspiracy-three-with-ties-to-dnc-mysteriously-die-n2203000

list[196] of questionable deaths that follows New York's Sixth Crime Family around like a bad odor. If we don't stand up after the Miracle in November and demand that the swamp is drained when will it happen? When Chelsea gets elected?

---

[195] *The Political Insider*, 6-25-19, accessed 6-19-19 https://thepoliticalinsider.com/another-clinton-associate-found-dead-bill-hillarys-body-count-increases/

[196] Accessed 6-19-19 https://www.freewebs.com/jeffhead/liberty/liberty/bdycount.txt

Drain the Swamp

Dispatch Twenty-seven

Republicrats Impeachment
and the Silent Coup

We have a three pronged attack aiming to reverse the results of last November's election. First comes the Government Party, let's call them the Republicrats, made up of the perpetually re-elected hacks who infest the capital of the world. Second is the deep state cancer that infects the federal bureaucracy. And third are the one world social democrats masquerading as journalists.

These three give their middle finger to America as they point their index fingers at President Trump. They accuse him of colluding with the Russians to steal the last election. And all the while they're colluding with leakers committing felonies and endangering American security in an effort to overthrow the President.

Drain the Swamp

A few things to illustrate the problem:

According to Adam Kredo of the Washington Free Beacon:[197]

A new wave of leaks targeting the Trump administration has actively endangered ongoing intelligence and military operations being conducted by the United States and its allies, sparking anger and concern inside and outside the White House, according to multiple conversations with senior U.S. officials intimately familiar with the situation.

The classified leaks, which are being handed to sympathetic journalists by former Obama administration officials who left the government and by holdovers still serving in the Trump administration, have damaged a number of ongoing operations, ranging from American efforts to prevent Russian infiltration of the United States to Israeli efforts against ISIS, sources said.

---

[197] Krdo, A., *The Washigton Free Beacon*, 6-26-17, accessed 6-19-19 https://freebeacon.com/national-security/anti-trump-leak-campaign-damaging-u-s-allied-operations/

According to Theodore Bunker of Newsmax:[198]

The FBI has seized smashed hard drives from the home of a Democratic House staffer an aide to Debbie Wasserman Schultz, The Daily Caller.[199]

Imran Awan, a longtime IT aide of Rep. Debbie Wasserman Schultz, D-Fla., is under investigation for allegedly stealing equipment and improperly accessing the House IT network, while working in Congress. Shortly after the case went public, Awan moved out of his home in Lorton, Virginia, renting it eventually to a couple, one a Marine Corps veteran and one a Navy Officer.

The renters told The Daily Caller they found "wireless routers, hard drives that look like they tried to destroy, laptops, [and] a lot of

---

[198] Bunker, T., *Newsmax*, 7-24-17, accessed 6-19-19 https://www.newsmax.com/Newsfront/private-email-server-hard-drives-FBI-investigation/2017/07/24/id/803506/

[199] Rosiak, L., *The Daily Caller*, 7-23-17, accessed 6-19-19 https://dailycaller.com/2017/07/23/exclusive-fbi-seized-smashed-hard-drives-from-wasserman-schultz-it-aides-home/

brand new expensive toner." They called the Naval Criminal Investigative Service, which coordinated with the FBI and Capitol Police to seize the equipment.

"It was in the garage. They recycled cabinets and lined them along the walls. They left in a huge hurry," the unnamed Marine, who spoke under the condition of anonymity out of concern for his wife's career, told The Daily Caller. "It looks like government-issued equipment. We turned that stuff over."

Democratic Rep. Debbie Wasserman Schultz has admitted that she violated official information security policy – blaming the chief administrative officer in the House of Representatives for not stopping her The Daily Caller.[200]

According to John Solomon of The Hill:[201]

---

[200] Rosiak, L., *The Daily Caller*, 5-31-17, accessed 6-19-19
https://dailycaller.com/2017/05/31/wasserman-schultz-admits-hill-it-security-violations-blames-house-administrators-for-not-stopping-her-video/
[201] Solomon, J., *The Hill*, 7-25-17, accessed 6-19-19
https://thehill.com/policy/national-security/343785-

Drain the Swamp

The National Security Agency and FBI violated specific civil liberty protections during the Obama administration by improperly searching and disseminating raw intelligence on Americans or failing to promptly delete unauthorized intercepts, according to newly declassified memos that provide some of the richest detail to date on the spy agencies' ability to obey their own rules.

The Hill reviewed the new ACLU documents as well as compliance memos released by the NSA inspector general and identified more than 90 incidents where violations specifically cited an impact on Americans. Many incidents involved multiple persons, multiple violations or extended periods of time.

For instance, the government admitted improperly searching the NSA's foreign intercept data on multiple occasions, including one instance in which an analyst ran the same search query about an

---

newly-declassified-memos-detail-extent-of-improper-obama-era-nsa

American "every work day" for a period between 2013 and 2014.

According to John Solomon of The Hill:[202]

The chairman of the House Intelligence Committee is accusing top political aides of President Obama of making hundreds of requests during the 2016 presidential race to unmask the names of Americans in intelligence reports, including Trump transition officials.

Intelligence Chairman Devin Nunes (R-Calif.), in a letter to the Director of National Intelligence Dan Coats, said the requests were made without specific justifications on why the information was needed.

"We have found evidence that current and former government officials had easy access to U.S. person information and that it is possible that they used this information to achieve partisan political purposes, including the selective, anonymous leaking

---

[202] Solomon, J., *The Hill*, 7-27-17, accessed 6-19-19 https://thehill.com/policy/national-security/343785-newly-declassified-memos-detail-extent-of-improper-obama-era-nsa

of such information," Nunes wrote in the letter to Coats.

The Obama 'Demasking' Scandal is not just growing, it's surging. Everyday more comes to light showing how the Obummber administration as it headed for the showers did their best to disseminate classified information as far afield as possible. Of course the ABCNBCCBSPBSCNNMASNBCNPR Cartel isn't going to tell the low-information voters anything about it and of course they won't do any research of their own. So I guess it's just between you and I and the millions who care to look.

According to Fred Fleitz of Newsmax:[203]

You wouldn't know it from the mainstream media, but the scandal of Obama officials weaponizing U.S. intelligence to collect against their political enemies is not just growing, it's surging.

There have been several damning reports over the last few weeks that Obama officials

---

[203] Fleitz, F., Newsmax, 8-2-17, accessed 6-19-19 https://www.newsmax.com/FredFleitz/clapper-national-intelligence/2017/08/02/id/805365/

made hundreds of requests to "demask" the names of Trump campaign and transition officials from intelligence reports. Some of these demasked names were leaked to the press to hurt Mr. Trump politically before and after the election.

And all this cloak and dagger skullduggery is leading up to one thing, the impeachment of President Trump. Since they've known from the beginning there was no collusion between the President and the Russians they have to find another way to thread the needle. The Special Counsel witch-hunt is frantically searching day and night to find anything to call a crime so they can get the ball rolling. And the political savants in Congress are doing their bit too. They're attempting to pass a bill, hopefully for them, with a veto proof majority that makes it a crime for the President to fire the Special Counsel. This is a replay of the same strategy used to impeach President Andrew Johnson.

In Johnson's case it was the Tenure of Office Act. The action of President Johnson that led directly to his impeachment was his deliberate violation of the Tenure of Office Act. The Tenure of Office Act was repealed in 1887. In 1926, the Supreme Court ruled that it was unconstitutional even though it had been repealed almost 40 years before.

So here we go again. How can it possibly make sense to pass a law saying that the head of the executive branch is committing a crime to fire someone who works for the executive branch? But that's where we're headed. If there is no crime they'll manufacture one.

According to Joe Crowe of Newsmax:[204]

A bipartisan (Republicrat) bill in the Senate would turn Department of Justice regulations about the president's ability to take action against a special counsel into law, according to Sen. Chris Coons, D-Del.

The bill would also require that an attorney general confirmed by the Senate would be

---

[204] Crowe, J., *Newsmax*, 8-7-17, accessed 6-19-19 https://www.newsmax.com/Politics/chris-coons-bill-special-counsel-robert-mueller/2017/08/07/id/806268/

the only official able to fire Mueller, according to Coons.

If for this or any other reason the House impeaches and the Senate removes President Trump we Deplorables out here in fly over country may see this whole election business for a sham. If we dare to elect someone who isn't one of the self-appointed crooked lawyers whose conflicts of interest are aided and abetted by the special interests the big bi-coastal pajama boys will just overturn our choice and go back to business as usual. Or so they think.

Dispatch Twenty-eight

North Korean Situation History
and Proposed Solution

Of course the current North Korean brouhaha is all Trump's fault at least according to the propaganda megaphone and prime time indoctrination machine that is the ABCCBSNBCPBSCNNMSNBCNPR Cartel. But then again according to these Alt-Left AntiFa stenographers what isn't?

To be effective all current events must happen in a vacuum. That way the spinmeisters can work their editorial magic and make everything fit their narrative.

Therefore in their delegitimizing playbook aimed at the eventual impeachment of President Trump the North Korean nuclear showdown is all because of Trump's bellicose rhetoric. However current events are the History of the Future and they need to be seen in context to be understood.

Way back in the mists of recorded time, on October 18, 1994 President Bill Clinton facing the reality of North Korea saying it was going to build nuclear weapons acted out the usual Democrat imitation of Nevil Chamberlain. In other words Mr. Clinton gave the tin-pot dictator de jure whatever desired as long as he could wave a little piece of paper and declare it signified "Peace in our time" just before an election.

He briefly described the "Deal" this way, "This agreement [$4 billion in U.S. energy aid] will help achieve a longstanding and vital American objective—an end to the threat of nuclear proliferation on the Korean Peninsula."[205]

Looking for a talking point to help the Democrat machine maintain its traditional hold on Congress Mr. Clinton set the North Koreans on the road to a nuclear bomb.

---

[205] Hunter, D., *Newsmax*, 8-4-17, accessed 6-19-19 https://www.newsmax.com/DavidLHunter/president-bill-clinton-north-korea-obama-iran/2017/08/14/id/807532/

Taking no thought for the eventual repercussions and looking only to immediate political advantage he threw America under the bus.

Even that flagship of the left the New York Times saw this for what it was, political maneuvering, not diplomacy. Here's how they described it at the time, "The accord struck in Geneva gave the President a chance to proclaim a major foreign policy success just weeks before the midterm election. But Asian diplomats pointed out today that it also placed the United States in the odd position of bolstering the political capital of a man it has regularly denounced as a terrorist, a supplier of missile technology to Iran and a dictator: Kim Jong Il."[206]

---

[206] Sanger, D., *The New York Times*, 10-19-94, accessed 6-19-19 https://www.nytimes.com/1994/10/19/world/clinton -approves-a-plan-to-give-aid-to-north- koreans.html?pagewanted=all&mtrref=undefined&g wh=F19255278F7637CB99797C6E191ACE85&gwt=p ay

Clinton said, "North Korea will freeze and then dismantle its nuclear program."[207]

Here's what the Times had to say, "What bothers some nuclear experts, from the Pentagon to the International Atomic Energy Agency, is that the North will continue to possess nuclear spent fuel for years, surrendering it only when the new reactors are nearing completion. That leaves open the possibility that if it ever renounced this week's agreement it could eject all international inspectors and resume the bomb project."[208]

According to President Clinton, "The United States and international inspectors will carefully monitor North Korea to make sure it keeps its commitments. Only as it does so

---

[207] Vespa, M., *Townhall*, 8-9-17, accessed 6-19-19 https://townhall.com/tipsheet/mattvespa/2017/08/09/that-time-bill-clinton-said-north-korea-will-dismantle-its-nuke-program-n1981099
[208] Sanger, D., *The New York Times*, 10-19-94, accessed 6-19-19 https://www.nytimes.com/1994/10/19/world/clinton-approves-a-plan-to-give-aid-to-north-koreans.html?pagewanted=all&mtrref=undefined&gwh=F19255278F7637CB99797C6E191ACE85&gwt=pay

will North Korea fully join the community of nations."[209]

As reported by the New York Times, "'This means that we are living with a country that flouted the Nuclear Nonproliferation Treaty and will remain in noncompliance for years,' an atomic energy agency official said today. 'We wanted to get that fuel out of the country, and out of the country fast.'"[210]

And, "'Similarly, some of the agency's officials are concerned that the so-called special inspection of a suspected nuclear site that they demanded two years ago -- a demand that prompted the North to announce it would pull out of the Nonproliferation Treaty -- will be delayed for five years or more. "It is not a good precedent to set,' the official said, 'if we

---

[209] Vespa, M., *Townhall*, 8-9-17, accessed 6-19-19 https://townhall.com/tipsheet/mattvespa/2017/08/0 9/that-time-bill-clinton-said-north-korea-will-dismantle-its-nuke-program-n1981099
[210] Sanger, D., *The New York Times*, 10-19-94, accessed 6-19-19 https://www.nytimes.com/1994/10/19/world/clinton -approves-a-plan-to-give-aid-to-north-koreans.html?pagewanted=all&mtrref=undefined&g wh=F19255278F7637CB99797C6E191ACE85&gwt=p ay

have to demand a special inspection in Iran or Iraq or someplace else in the world."'[211]

The Times had a bit more to say about this American Munich, "President Clinton approved a plan today to arrange more than $4 billion in energy aid to North Korea during the next decade in return for a commitment from the country's hardline Communist leadership to freeze and gradually dismantle its nuclear weapons development program."[212]

And, "American and North Korean officials plan to sign the broad accord on Friday, and almost immediately the United States will begin a remarkable new foreign aid program: it will provide for the North, with which it has never signed a peace treaty ending the Korean War, supplies of heavy oil to keep factories running and homes heated."[213]

And not only did the United States agree to provide oil Bill Clinton arranged for something else, "The accord calls for a

---

[211] Ibid.
[212] Ibid.
[213] Ibid.

consortium of nations, led by South Korea and Japan, to provide the North with two light-water nuclear reactors, designed in a manner that makes it far more difficult for the North to convert nuclear waste into atomic weapons."

I wonder what the Kim dynasty has done with those reactors?[214]

Along come George II and what does he do? He inaugurates the Six Party Talks between the United States, South and North Korea, China, Russia, and Japan. These talks went on and off for years eventually producing nothing but more time for North Korea to improve upon their first nuclear test which happened on the second Bush watch.

The Obama Administration courageously followed a policy of strategic patience,[215] essentially a commitment to denuclearization as a precondition for talks, conducted in close alliance with Seoul and the other members of the Six-Party Talks.

---

[214] Ibid.
[215] Gard, R., *The Diplomat*, 11-21-13, accessed 6-19-19 https://thediplomat.com/2013/11/strategic-patience-with-north-korea/

Drain the Swamp

The talks continued to drag on as Mr. Obama kicked the can down the road.

Now the latest model of a crazy Kim struts around like a bantam rooster with a bad haircut on the world stage. He overtly threatens us with nuclear war and President Trump stands up to him.

To the corporations once known as the mainstream media this is provocative. Standing up for yourself is not the progressive way. We are supposed to cower in the corner and apologize for being who we are. That is not the American way. At least it wasn't before the Clinton – Bush – Obama era.

As stated earlier: To be effective all current events must happen in a vacuum. That way the spinmeisters can work their editorial magic and make everything fit their narrative.

However, nothing happens in a vacuum. We must consider the context for a text without a context is a pretext.

So how are we supposed to deal with North Korea short of turning them into a sea of glass?

I propose that we pull our troops out of South Korea. With a population twice as large and an economy almost four times the size of the stunted North the South should be able to fend for itself after 67 years of American protection. Then we tell China that unless they reign in their protégé we will help South Korea, Japan, and Taiwan to build their own nuclear weapons. Then we step aside and let the Asian Tigers figure out how to bell the cat in Pyongyang.

Drain the Swamp

Dispatch Twenty-nine

A Convention of the States
What Are They Afraid Of?

The Founders had one great fear; that a time would come when the Federal Government would overstep its bounds and come to dominate the individual States. Can anyone reading this dispute that this is such a time?

Look at our State governments. They are so addicted to Federal money they can't exist without it. And they can't get it without enough strings attached to turn them into little more than marionettes. They prance upon the stage masquerading as independent actors. In reality almost every step, every hand movement, every program, policy, and mandate is choreographed in the imperial capital.

The Founders saw this coming from more than 200 years away. And they made a provision for it.

Article V of the Constitution states:

The Congress, whenever two thirds of both houses shall deem it necessary, shall propose amendments to this Constitution, or, on the application of the legislatures of two thirds of the several states, shall call a convention for proposing amendments, which, in either case, shall be valid to all intents and purposes, as part of this Constitution, when ratified by the legislatures of three fourths of the several states, or by conventions in three fourths thereof, as the one or the other mode of ratification may be proposed by the Congress; provided that no amendment which may be made prior to the year one thousand eight hundred and eight shall in any manner affect the first and fourth clauses in the ninth section of the first article; and that no state, without its consent, shall be deprived of its equal suffrage in the Senate.

Drain the Swamp

In January of 2016 Governor Greg Abbott of Texas issued call for a Convention of the States. He advanced what is known as the Texas plan asking for the consideration of the following amendments to the U.S. Constitution:

Prohibit Congress from regulating activity that occurs wholly within one state.

Require Congress to balance the federal budget.

Prohibit administrative agencies from creating federal law.

Prohibit administrative agencies from pre-empting state law.

Allow a two-thirds majority of the states to override a U.S. Supreme Court decision.

Require a seven-justice supermajority vote for U.S. Supreme Court decisions that invalidate a democratically enacted law.

Limit federal powers to those expressly delegated in the Constitution.

Give state officials the power to sue in federal court when federal officials overstep their bounds.

Allow a two-thirds majority of the states to override a federal law or regulation.

This call for action has inspired outrage and fear. Why?

Ever since the ratification of the Seventeenth Amendment in 1913 changed the election of Senators, originally been elected by State legislators, to popular election the States have had no representation in Washington. This changed the relationship and nature of our federal system. The House was created to represent the people. The Senate was created to represent the States. Now with the popular election of Senators every State hires lobbyists to represent their interests. They've lost their voice.

The amendments by the governor of Texas would go a long way to redressing the balance. We need to do something to rein a runaway federal behemoth that's smothering all of us under its stifling regulations.

The Progressives have been vocal in their resistance to the idea of a Convention of the States. They contend that they don't want anyone messing with the Constitution. This is especially ironic since it's the Progressives and the evolution of a Living Document that have brought us to this point. They've used the courts and the bureaucracy to change the Constitution without amending it.

President Woodrow Wilson, the quintessential Progressive, openly declared the Constitution an impediment to the kinds of reforms the Progressive Movement wanted. So he urged judges to interpret the Constitution in such a way as to loosen its limits on federal power. And he tried to use the bureaucracy to regulate freedom into serfdom.

The Progressives have been complaining for years that amending the Constitution is too hard. That is why we need a Living Document that can change with the times. That is why we needed to change that which was written in stone to that which is written in the sand.

It was supposed to be hard to amend the Constitution. That was one of the checks and balances written into the original document to help maintain the limited government it was written to establish and maintain. So instead of seeking to amend the Progressives have depended on federal judges especially Supreme Court justices to amend the Constitution through court rulings and precedence in a leftward direction.

For generations this unconstitutional judicial amendment process has continued step-by-step inch-by-inch until today government officials at the local, state or national level can seize private property in disregard of the 5th Amendment's protections. They can listen to and record everything we say in contravention of the 4th Amendment. They disregard the14th Amendment's provision of equal protection under the law allowing government-imposed group preferences and quotas under the name of affirmative action. Our celebrated equal rights have been sacrificed on the altar of diversity.

It's a lie repeated enough to be accepted as true that the federal courts are merely interpreting the Constitution rather than re-writing it when they discover new rights that aren't there and disregard ones that are.

The claim of the Progressives that this dishonest process is necessary because it's so difficult to formally amend the Constitution is exposed as a lie by the success of their own movement. When their movement was young, before they invented the Living Document and the judicial interpretation process of change the Constitution was amended four times in just eight years. In all it has been formally amended 27 times.

So why is it so threatening to some people to call a Convention of States to propose amendments to the Constitution?

Let's look at this logically. Why is this so threatening?

From a legal standpoint it isn't some radical invention of the Alt-right. The Constitution lists a convention of states as one of the ways that amendments can be officially proposed. True it has never yet been done. But does that mean it is suspect or dangerous? Remember it takes two-thirds of the States to call a Convention and any proposed amendments put forward will need the votes of three-fourths of the States to be ratified. What's so radical about that?

Here are my questions for those who fear a Convention of the States: Would you rather have the Constitution changed by a 5 to 4 vote of the Supreme Court? Would you rather have the Constitution changed by the rulings of a lone federal judge? Would you rather have the Constitution changed by the rulings of the Ninth Circuit? Would you rather have it changed by the unilateral actions of a president? Or would you rather have it changed by the administrative rulings of faceless bureaucrats in federal agencies?

Many express the fear that a Convention of the States would repeat History. The original Constitutional Convention was called by Congress to propose amendments to the Articles of Confederation. Instead the Framers locked themselves in and wrote the Constitution in secret. Then they presented it to the States for ratification. The congress under the Articles eventually agreed to its own dissolution when public opinion showed a majority wanted the new government as proposed. This is the basis of the fear even if many do not know the whole story.

This fear overlooks the fact that it takes the votes of two-thirds of the states to call for a convention. And it takes three-fourths of the states to actually pass an amendment. Therefore, nothing could happen that was not the expression of the overwhelming majority of the representatives of the people.

Instead of a radical assault upon the Constitution

Gov. Abbott's proposed amendments would restore constitutional protections that have

241

been eroded and/or erased by unelected federal judges, by imperial presidents, and by unelected bureaucrats in administrative agencies.

We the People are being kept out of the process. Why? What are the Progressives and their media machine afraid of?

Though the Progressives consistently portray themselves through their media megaphone as the champions of the people, using the tactics of judicial overreach, legislative slight-of-hand, and bureaucratic fiat they continuously work to remove decisions from the hands of citizens. Instead they deliver us like lambs to the slaughter to unelected federal judges and faceless bureaucrats with civil service job protection and golden parachutes.

Is it any wonder that the Progressives don't want us to have a convention that could possibly restore the Constitution as the guarantee of limited government, individual liberty, and economic opportunity for all?

Drain the Swamp

Dispatch Thirty

Why Are Unions Against the Right-to-Work?

I come from a union family. I grew up in a union home. The good pay and benefits gained by one of America's greatest unions provided for my room and board every day that I lived at home. My father and my uncles were all proud union members. My brother and some of my best friends spent their entire careers as union workers and the unions are providing them with generous pensions and great benefits. I myself was at one time the Vice President of an International Union. For all of this I am grateful.

The right to organize is a time honored American tradition and one that I believe is guaranteed by the First Amendment to the Constitution which states, "Congress shall make no law respecting an establishment of religion, or prohibiting the free exercise thereof; or abridging the freedom of speech, or of the press; or the right of the people peaceably to assemble, and to petition the Government for a redress of grievances." Peaceable assembly is the hallmark of American union organizing.

Some of the things we take for granted were won for us through the organization of labor in unions. Unions helped establish the concept of the weekend. Unions helped establish fair wages and relative income equality. Unions helped end child labor. Unions helped to stablish widespread employer-based health coverage. Here are a few others that can be attributed either wholly or at least partly to the impact of unions in America's workplace: Paid Vacation, Sick Leave, 8-Hour Work Day, Overtime Pay, 40 Hour Work Week, Worker's Compensation, Pensions, Holiday Pay, and Military Leave. That's a pretty long and impressive list isn't it?

I will always be the first among any to say that Unions have had a beneficial impact on American life. I will also say that the contest between the rights of workers and the rights of employers has swung like a pendulum back and forth several times and whenever it swings too hard to the employer side it is unions and organizing that gives workers the best chance to redress the balance.

Having said all this I believe I stand on solid ground when I say that I am not anti-union.

This brings me to the question that serves as the title of this column, "Why are unions against the right-to-work?"

That unions are universally opposed to right to work laws is well documented in the media. Listen to the two largest American Unions. From the AFL-CIO web site, ""Right to work" is the name for a policy designed to take away rights from working people."[216] On their web site the Teamsters put it this way, "Right to work is wrong for working people."[217] The supporters of the union war against right to

---

[216] AFL-CIO, accessed 6-19-19
https://aflcio.org/issues/right-work
[217] Teamsters, accessed 6-19-19
https://teamster.org/news/2017/02/teamsters-strongly-oppose-national-right-work-legislation

work legislation say such things as: "This type of deregulation cripples the right to organize a union."[218] "Right-to-work laws require workers and their unions to cover the costs of non-union workers who benefit from union contracts. These laws are proven to drive down wages and weaken workers' unions by undercutting bargaining power."[219] And "The real purpose of right to work laws is to tilt the balance toward big corporations and further rig the system at the expense of working families."[220]

This debate has been going on for a long time. James Sherk of Heritage Foundation laid out the union's objections and the rebuttal of Libertarians quite well back in 2014:[221]

---

[218] Left Voice, 2-2-17, accessed 6-19-19
https://www.leftvoice.org/The-Unions-Must-Fight-Against-Right-to-Work
[219] Teamsters, accessed 6-19-19
https://teamster.org/news/2017/02/teamsters-strongly-oppose-national-right-work-legislation
[219] *Left Voice*, 2-2-17, accessed 6-19-19
[220] AFL-CIO, accessed 6-19-19
https://aflcio.org/issues/right-work
[221] Sherk, J., The Heritage Foundation, 12-12-14, accessed 6-19-19 https://www.heritage.org/jobs-and-labor/report/right-work-laws-myth-vs-fact

Myth: *Right-to-work laws prohibit unions.*

Fact: *Right-to-work laws make union dues voluntary.* Without right-to-work laws, unions negotiate contracts that force workers to pay dues or get fired. Right-to-work laws protect workers' freedom. The National Labor Relations Act also protects the right of workers in right-to-work states to unionize. Unions currently represent 4.4 million workers in 24 right-to-work states, including highly unionized Nevada, Iowa, and Michigan.

Myth: *Right-to-work laws undermine unions.*

Fact: *Right-to-work laws make unions work to earn workers' support.* In the long run, this can strengthen union locals. Without right-to-work laws, unions can take their members' dues for granted and provide lower quality representation. Gary Casteel, the Southern region director for the United Auto Workers, explains:

This is something I've never understood, that people think right to work hurts unions.

To me, it helps them. You don't have to belong if you don't want to. So if I go to an organizing drive, I can tell these workers, "If you don't like this arrangement, you don't have to belong." Versus, "If we get 50 percent of you, then all of you have to belong, whether you like to or not." I don't even like the way that sounds, because it's a voluntary system, and if you don't think the system's earning its keep, then you don't have to pay.

Myth: *Right-to-work laws allow non-union members to "free ride" on the benefits of union representation without paying its cost.*

Fact: *Unions voluntarily represent non-members.* The Supreme Court has repeatedly ruled that the National Labor Relations Act allows unions to negotiate contracts covering only dues-paying members. As Justice Brennan wrote in *Retail Clerks v. Dry Lion Goods* (1962), "'Members only' contracts have long been recognized." Unions represent non-members only when they act as "exclusive bargaining representatives," which requires non-members to accept the union's representation. In that case, the law requires unions to represent non-members fairly. They cannot negotiate high wages for their supporters and the minimum wage for non-members. Unions can avoid representing non-members by disclaiming exclusive representative status.

Myth: *Representing non-members costs exclusive representative unions a lot of money.*

Fact: *Unions often spend little on representational activities.* When unions choose to act as exclusive bargaining representatives, they often spend relatively little on processing grievances and negotiating contracts. Often union contracts have employers cover these costs by allowing union stewards to do union business while on company time. As a result, many union locals spend very little representing workers—either members or non-members.

Federal filings reveal that in 2013 United Auto Workers Local 2164 in Bowling Green, Kentucky, spent just 2 percent of its

$560,000 budget on representational activities. Boilermakers Local 107 in Brookfield, Wisconsin, spent 5 percent of its $2.0 million budget on representational activities. Machinists Lodge 2515 in Alamogordo, New Mexico, spent 23 percent of its $645,000 budget on representational activities—almost all of which constituted payments to its officers.

Myth: *Right-to-work laws provide no economic benefits.*

Fact: *Companies consider right-to-work laws a major factor when deciding where to locate.* Organizing victories bring in a lot more money for a union in jurisdictions with compulsory dues. Consequently, unions organize more aggressively in places without right-to-work laws. Companies in turn want to know they can avoid being targeted by union organizers if they treat their workers well. Right-to-work laws make that more likely. Economic development consultant's report that roughly half of all major businesses refuse to consider locating in jurisdictions with compulsory dues. Bureau of Labor

Statistics data show that between 1990 and 2014 total employment grew more than twice as fast in right-to-work states as in states with compulsory dues.

Myth: *Right-to-work laws lower wages.*

Fact: *Workers have the same or higher buying power in right-to-work states.* Opponents often deride voluntary dues as "right-to-work for less." Average wages in right-to-work states are indeed slightly lower than in non-right-to-work states. This occurs because almost every Southern state has a right-to-work law and the South has a lower cost of living. Studies that control for differences in costs of living find workers in states with voluntary dues have no lower— and possibly slightly higher—real wages than workers in states with compulsory dues.

Myth: *Right-to-work laws divide Americans.*

Fact: *Americans overwhelmingly support right-to-work laws.* Recent Gallup polling finds Americans support right-to-work laws by a 71 percent to 22 percent margin—better than 3 to 1. Independents support right-to-work laws 77 percent to 17 percent, Republicans support them 74 percent to 18 percent, and Democrats support them 65 percent to 30 percent. Polling also shows that union members themselves support voluntary dues by an 80 percent to 17 percent margin. Voters also reward politicians who support voluntary dues at the polls. Not a single Michigan legislator who voted for right-to-work laws in 2012 lost in the next general election. Right-to-work laws remain controversial primarily among union officers—not the general public.

The arguments against right-to-work laws do not withstand scrutiny. Right-to-work laws give workers a choice over where their money goes. This freedom forces unions to earn their members' support. It also attracts businesses and jobs. The law should not force anyone in America to pay union dues as a condition of employment.

I have a few questions for union members who follow their unions lead and oppose right-to-work. Can anyone join? Is it open to all people at all times or is union membership restricted in any way? If membership is restricted isn't this a restraint of trade? Are union wages artificially high because they only allow so many people to compete for jobs?

Personally I believe every citizen deserves the right to work and the right to organize and I don't believe they should be mutually exclusive. Unions should not need government coercion to exist and workers shouldn't need to bust unions to work.

Now here's a wild idea in the current atmosphere of confrontation and battle that is drowning America why don't we have a civil debate about this and then let the voters decide.

Dispatch Thirty-one

The Trump Agenda What We Voted For

Remember the campaign? Trump leapt in front of a parade that began in 2009 with the birth of the TEA Party Movement. The Trump campaign embodied everything those who wanted America to recover from the Obama debacle desired. What it proclaimed, what we were promised was an end to open borders, a repeal and replace of Obamacare, tax reform, and an end to give-away trade deals that have impoverished and debilitated us. In other words an America First administration supported by a do-something Congress.

And what have we gotten for our vote? The RINOs led by Ryan, McConnell, McCain, Flake, and Graham continue to obstruct everything President Trump tries to do. No repeal and replace. No tax reform, no support on the immigrant ban, and no support in stopping the bogus Russian-under-every -table investigation.

The Republicans said they needed the House to stop Obama. We gave them the House and they said they needed the Senate too. We gave them both houses of Congress and they did nothing to stop Obama. They said they needed the Presidency and then they could do something to right the ship-of-state. We gave them the presidency and since then it's become obvious these political hacks were stringing us along all along.

We need to hold their feet to the fire. Call them. Email them. Show up at their town meetings. Let them know we want them to make America great again. Let them know we want what we voted for. We want an America First government.

I doubt that any amount of lobbying by those of us in fly-over country will have any impact on the crooked lawyers and others who hold the levers of power no matter what political shell-game party they say they belong to. There is only one party in

Congress and it's a two-headed bird of prey out to eat our lunch.

Watch for an acceleration of the witch hunt. Watch for movement on the impeachment front. Watch for a complete sell-out of everything we voted for in the interests of what the special interests paid for.

The AntiFa Blackshirts and other bully boys who serve as the shock troops for the silent coup will not stop until there's blood in the water. The ABCCBSNBCPBSNPRCNNMSNBC Cartel will continue to cover-up the truth and proclaim the lie. The Neocons have re-captured our foreign policy and are driving us towards the cliff.

It's time for all of us who voted for President Trump to prepare for the counter-revolution. Like Charley Brown trying to kick the football we keep on trying and trying no matter how many times they move the ball. America, the greatest experiment in freedom in human history is worth trying to save from the statists and their collective fever dreams of utopia.

Drain the Swamp

Now is the time for all patriots to come to the aid of their country. Make your voice heard. Raise your hand and vote by participating in the process for making America great again.

Keep the faith. Keep the peace. We shall overcome.

Dispatch Thirty-two

Make America Great Again

I know a very intelligent man who says, "All politicians lie, the good ones do it convincingly."

The Donald won his miraculous victory based on promises that built an agenda to make America great again. These promises basically said that he would address three areas, the economy, the wall, and taxes. How's he doing so far?

The S&P 500 has added more than two trillion in market value since Trump's election.[222] This is an astounding run for a bull market. Records have been broken, and broken, and then broken again.

---

[222] Imbert, F., CNBC, 9-12-19, accessed 6-20-19 https://www.cnbc.com/2017/09/12/sp-500s-value-has-soared-by-2-trillion-since-donald-trump-election.html

I call this the Trump Bump.

Economy growing: check.

What about the wall?

Homeland Security has issued a waiver to certain laws, regulations and other legal requirements to ensure the expeditious construction of barriers in the vicinity of the international border near Calexico, California.[223] The waiver was published in the Federal Register today so construction of the border wall can begin.

How can this be? I thought from hearing the media cartels storyline that this would never happen.

In legislation already on the books Congress provided the Secretary of Homeland Security with a number of authorities necessary to carry out its border security mission.

---

[223] Homeland Security, 8-1-17, accessed 6-20-19 https://www.dhs.gov/news/2017/08/01/dhs-issues-waiver-expedite-border-construction-projects-san-diego-area

Current law provides that the Secretary of Homeland Security shall take such actions as may be necessary to install additional physical barriers and roads in the vicinity of the United States border to deter illegal crossings in areas of high illegal entry into the United States. In laws already in effect Congress called for the installation of additional fencing, barriers, roads, lighting, cameras, and sensors on the southwest border. In this legislation Congress granted to the Secretary of Homeland Security the authority to waive all legal requirements that the Secretary, in his sole discretion, determines necessary to ensure the expeditious construction of the barriers and roads authorized.

DHS is implementing President Trump's Executive Order 13767, Border Security and Immigration Enforcement Improvements, enforcing laws already on the books laws that've been unenforced for years and is taking steps to immediately plan, design and construct a physical wall along the southern border, using appropriate materials and technology to most effectively achieve complete operational control of the border.

In other words despite the fake news the Corporations Once Known as the Mainstream Media keep spinning President Trump is moving forward with his promise to build the wall.

Wall underway: Check.

What about taxes?

For years I've predicted that if we would reform the bewildering tax code, personally I advocate for a flat tax of 15%, lower the corporate tax, allow the repatriation of foreign holdings, and scale back regulation our economy would take off like a rocket. The Trump administration is eliminating sixteen regulations for every new one. Throw tax reform into the mix and maybe we're about to see if that prediction has been valid. Two trillion in growth may pale in comparison to what Americans can do if we remove the shackles forged by the anti-capitalist Progressives over the last twenty-nine years.

If we can corral enough RINOs we can pass the president's tax reform plan.[224]

Donald Trump promised that if we elected him together we would make America great again. Since the day of his election he's been under assault by the establishment. It's been unrelenting and according to the latest survey coverage has been 91% negative.[225] It's become so ludicrous that if the President walked on water the headline would be, "Trump can't swim!" If he changed water into wine it would be, "Trump encourages alcoholism!" And if he raised the dead it would be, "Trump attacks the funeral parlor industry!"

Even the politically blind can see through this haze of bias and partisanship disguised as journalism. Even those made deaf by Progressive indoctrination disguised as education can hear that the political hacks

---

[224] Pavich, K., *Townhall*, 9-27-17, accessed 6-20-19 https://townhall.com/tipsheet/katiepavlich/2017/09/27/here-is-president-trumps-full-tax-reform-plan-n2387522
[225] *World Net Daily*, 9-12-17, accessed 6-20-19 https://www.wnd.com/2017/09/study-trump-news-coverage-91-negative/

and their media megaphone are doing a hatchet job on a man who sacrificed a life as a successful entrepreneur to work a thankless job for the benefit of his country.

Why? What could induce someone to leave a life of luxury surrounded by a loving family all working together to accomplish great things? Why would one of the most successful builders in American history leave his own plans in the hands of others to take on a job draining a swamp? Why give up the life of a super star idolized and lionized by millions to be caricatured and hated by those driven mad because they didn't get their way?

Why?

To make America great again that's why.

Remember the man who said, "All politicians lie, the good ones do it convincingly." My vote went to a non-politician because I hoped a businessman might tell me the truth.

Let's dedicate ourselves to doing anything and everything we can to support the President in his goal. Contact your

Drain the Swamp

Senators. Call your Representative. Let them know that you want them to help not hinder the President. Let them know you want them to forget about getting themselves re-elected and instead work to Make America Great Again!

Drain the Swamp

Dispatch Thirty-three

Build the Wall Build the Wall Build the Wall

President Trump's speech before the UN
was interesting in many ways.[226]

He put the multinational globalists on
official notice that he has their number and
as far as he's concerned their number is up.
He let the UN bureaucrats know that their
red tape parades have got to be reined
in.[227] He called socialism what it is, a
failure.[228] He held up capitalism as the
means for raising people out of poverty and
ignorance. He made the case for
sovereignty both national, personal, and

---

[226] Youtube, accessed 6 20 19
https://www.youtube.com/watch?v=4KIpnPapquY
[227] Shaw, A., *Breitbart*, 9-18-19, accessed 6-20-19
[228] Saavedra, R., *The Daily Wire*, 9-19-17. Accessed
6-20-19
https://www.dailywire.com/news/21306/watch-
trump-slams-socialism-un-world-leaders-ryan-
saavedra

individual freedom.[229] He pointed out that the US carries a disproportionate load[230] for the support of the UN and that this has got to change or they might be looking for spare change if America cuts its funding for what has become an anti-American debating society.[231] In other words, he let the world know that as far as his administration is concerned from now on it's going to be America First.

He laid out some markers in foreign affairs for North Korea, Syria, Iran and Venezuela. He avoided platitudes and spoke bluntly of his thoughts about some of the disastrous deals made by previous administrations that empowered and inspired our enemies just as they discouraged our allies. He let

---

[229] De Haldevang, M., *Quartz*, 9-19-17, accessed 6-20-19 https://qz.com/1081499/unga-2017-trump-mentioned-sovereignty-21-times-in-a-speech-heralding-a-new-american-view-of-the-world/
[230] Schaefer, B., Fox News, 6-16-15, accessed 6-20-19 https://qz.com/1081499/unga-2017-trump-mentioned-sovereignty-21-times-in-a-speech-heralding-a-new-american-view-of-the-world/
[231] Shaw, A., *Breitbart*, 9-18-19, accessed 6-20-19 https://www.breitbart.com/politics/2017/09/18/trump-gives-stern-warning-u-n-reform-says-potential-marred-bureaucracy-mismanagement/

everyone know he felt free to abort or amend these deals with American interests in mind this time.

The first speech at the UN is a right-of-passage for all new presidents. President Trump speaking to a room full of collectivist socialists pointed out such realities as the problem in Venezuela isn't that socialism hasn't been properly implemented the problem is that it's been implemented at all.[232] He was forthright and presented a good argument that freedom and capitalism is a superior system to coercion and socialism. For all this we should celebrate and give thanks that President Trump won in November 2016.

In the last election we had the choice between the last nail in our coffin and a chance. We now have a chance. America's place on the world stage is being clarified by President Trump. But we need to keep things in perspective.

---

[232] Feldscher, K. *The Washington Examiner*, 9-19-17, accessed 6-20-19 https://www.washingtonexaminer.com/trump-venezuela-in-crisis-because-socialism-has-been-faithfully-implemented

We need to keep our eye on the prize. What good will it do to gain the world if we lose the homeland? It was mainly domestic issues that drove everyone to the polls to prevent Hillary's coronation. We want America back not the globalist collective the Progressives have been shoving down our throat.

Stop the migration invasion. Secure the border. No amnesty. Bring our troops home from around the world and let them make us secure. Build the wall, build the wall, build the wall.

Those who say we cannot build a wall need to take a look at the border between North and South Korea.[233] It may not be a smaller version of the Great Wall but it's effective. Or look at the wall Israel built on their border with the Palestinian Authority.[234] If these secure borders can be

---

[233] Google, Korean DMZ, accessed 6-20-19
https://www.google.com/search?q=korea+dmz&tbm
=isch&tbo=u&source=univ&sa=X&ved=0ahUKEwiW1
eCy9bPWAhUP2mMKHTXkBAAQiR4ItAE&biw=1333&b
ih=618
[234] Google, Israeli Wall, accessed 6-20-19
https://www.google.com/search?q=israeli+wall&tbm
=isch&tbo=u&source=univ&sa=X&ved=0ahUKEwit4p

built, guarded, and maintained why can't we do the same thing on our Southern border?

Bring our troops home from Korea. Why should they be there as a trip wire? Their deaths are meant to do nothing else but guarantee that we'll be involved in the next war. Let South Korea, Japan, and Taiwan deal with the suicidal Rocket Man. Their populations and economies are much larger than the gulag which is North Korea.

Bring our troops home from Germany. Lately the Germans and French seem friendlier to Russia than they do to us so who are we protecting them from? Themselves?

Why should we spend billions each year to maintain these garrison troops left over from wars fought more than a half century ago. Instead of spending that money overseas post the troops to our southern border and spend that money in our own country.

Tb9bPWAhVD8WMKHYz7AO8QiR4IrwE&biw=1333&bih=618

DACA is a Trojan horse. Give amnesty to anyone and you'll end up giving it to everyone. The minute it becomes law the ACLU, CAIR, LA Raza and all the other America Last front groups will file challenges to the law's supposedly iron-clad limitations. These inevitable law suits will give liberal activist judges the opportunity to prop the door open. They'll argue, "Why is it fair that some get citizenship and others don't?" If the Trump Administration dares to stand against these attempts to stretch a limited amnesty into a come-one-come-all free-for-all the Ninth Circuit will get the opportunity to slap them down and knock the door off its hinges.

President Trump, for standing up to the globalists in their lair you are to be commended. Out here in fly-over country most are proud to hear you speak for us bravely and forthrightly to these representatives of demagogues and dictators.

But please, keep your eye on the prize. If you reform the Obamacare health insurance debacle, reform taxes, and cut regulations

Drain the Swamp

you'll go down as one of the greatest presidents in our history. However, when a patient is hemorrhaging the first thing to do is stop the bleeding. So first of all as our Commander-in-Chief, the one charged with protecting the nation, build the wall build the wall, build the wall.

Dispatch Thirty-four

Drain the Swamp

In America today most people choose their favorite brand of the radical leftist echo chamber ABCCBSNBCCNNMSNBCPBSNPR Cartel based on the charisma of the news reader, and don't waste their time tuning into any other news options.

What are the criteria for their choice of a news outlet? Does the news reader look or sound authoritative? Are they better looking? Do they have a more pleasing voice? Are they male? Are they female? Are they Gay? Are we not sure? Whatever the reason, it isn't because they say anything different. It often sounds like they all have the same writers and story selectors. The content is no different.

Do you want to hear the story about how the Republicrat Elite is going to stop the

Drain the Swamp

Trump agenda before or after you hear the story about how the Donald is not fit for the highest office in the land or after? Do you want to learn about the latest polls that show everyone hates Trump before or after you hear how Trump the Traitor colluded with the Russians before or after you hear about the insane proposals of the racist homophobe misogynist Trump to build a wall, stop the terrorists from moving next door, or starve the poor? Perhaps the line-up of the stories is slightly changed from one news clone to another but that's about it. All hate Trump all the time.

When I have a chance encounter and what passes for conversation with so many Kool-Aid drinking low information voters i.e progressive induhviduals the conversation usually goes like this:

Me: What do you think about _____ (fill in the blank)?

Progressive Induhvidual: Repeat what ABC, CBS, NBC, CNN, MSNBC, PBS, NPR, the New York Times, the Washington Post, USA Today, the Chicago Tribune, etc. has said recently stated as if this was their independently arrived at personal opinion.

Or if they're a Conservative Induhvidual: Repeat what Fox, the Wall Street Journal, the Weekly Standard, National Review, etc. has recently said.

It's almost impossible to find anyone who has actually read any books on topics of importance such as economics, politics, sociology, or the History that ties them all together.

Several times a year I attend meetings that are filled with nothing but PhDs, professors, and university administrators. All content experts in these very subjects as well as many others. The results are basically the same. The death of critical thinking has led to a deafening silence in the area of actual personal opinion, a dearth of dialogue, and a collapse of conversation.

The American people, who at the time of the Founding saw blacksmiths discussing with candle makers the pros and cons of constitutions and the meaning of liberty or carpenters debating with plumbers the need for a free economy versus the need for public works. Just read the Federalist and the Anti-Federalist Papers, look at the level of thought and speech and ask yourself, "How do the public debate, and newspaper articles of contemporary America match up?" Today the public debate takes place at about a 3rd grade level compared to the graduate school of those earlier days.

What happened? Back then there weren't public schools. Churches and families educated their own. Today after generations of highly funded and severely structured public education we've successfully dumbed ourselves down to the lowest common denominator.

Look at the late great Bernie Sanders revolt which was short circuited and contained by the ballot fixing elite in the Democrat Party. Or look at the Trump Revolution which overwhelmed the elite in the Republican Party. Either way it's obvious that we tax paying entities who inhabit flyover country whether of the right or left have had enough of the bi-coastal elite that's driving us over the cliff into the third world. Since their favorite empty pantsuit blew the election and she can't carry the water for the donor class all the way to the bank obviously the elite controlled media has dropped their camouflage of objectivity and is all in to make sure Trump is destroyed.

At least there was one pseudo surprise in the Hollywood scripted replay of Primary Colors the Distaff Edition. After all of the frothing at the mouth Bernie supporters did. After his highly motivated supporters were so brave they booed or turned their backs at the Democrat Party Spectacle in Philadelphia on their anointed queen. Low and behold their fearless leader fell into line and surprise, surprise, surprise supported the mistress of manipulation. Then just as evidence surfaced that yes, the entire primary exercise was rigged from the beginning the mind-numb robots of the left who chanted and cheered for Bernie stood in line to cast their rationally considered and highly principled vote for the very person who engineered the fix, took her money and marching orders from the crony capitalists, and is arguably the most corrupt person to ever run for the presidency. After the primary, Bernie, the man of the people bought his third house[235] and settled in a well feathered bed until next time he's needed to attack his fellow millionaires and billionaires.[236]

Who could have seen this coming except a blind man in a dark room with no media access?

The pre-programmed electorate combined with the usual fraud, imported voters and all the dead[237] people[238] who never leave[239] the voting rolls of the corrupt Democrat City fiefdoms, marched in lockstep to the polls to

---

[235] Nguyen, T., *Vanity Fair*, 8-9-16, accessed 6-20-19
https://www.vanityfair.com/news/2016/08/bernie-sanders-summer-house
[236] Schwab, N., *Daily Mail*, 6-5-17, accessed 6-20-19
https://www.dailymail.co.uk/news/article-4574760/Socialism-rewarding-s-Bernie-millionaire.html
[237] Goldstein, D., CBS, 5-23-16, accessed6-20-19
https://losangeles.cbslocal.com/2016/05/23/cbs2-investigation-uncovers-votes-being-cast-from-grave-year-after-year/
[238] Ballotpedia, accessed 6-20-19
https://ballotpedia.org/Dead_people_voting
[239] *World Net Daily*, 5-24-16, accessed 6-20-19
https://www.wnd.com/2016/05/hundreds-of-dead-voters-cast-ballots-decades-after-dying/

hand America lock-stock-and-barrel to the Clinton Crime Family.[240]

However the November Miracle happened and instead of the Sleazy Don following the totally corrupt Donna back into the White House the Donald won.

Enough people swallowed the red pill and were willing to at least take a shot at shaking things up before we're swept away by the unregulated immigration invasion and state sponsored outsourcing that low and behold we didn't end up with another perpetually re-elected hack.

An old saying goes, "There are only two things that are certain in this life, death and taxes." We've all been programmed to accept this as an inevitable truism. Death to be sure is natural and inevitable. If you were born you'll die. Taxes however aren't a natural thing. They're in actuality the forced expropriation of funds from the

---

[240] Murdock, D., *National Review*, 5-27-16, accessed 6-20-19
https://www.nationalreview.com/2016/05/hillary-clinton-bill-clinton-crime-family-where-politics-and-mafia-meet/

productive taken through the use of the state's monopoly on the use of coercive force. And so, though they aren't natural and they aren't inevitable like death or gravity they may in realistic terms given the overwhelming preponderance of government power be unavoidable.

Our country refused to follow the dictates of the elite controlled media. America refused to become the turf of the Sleazy Donna from Chappaqua whose word parsing motto should be the Bart Simpson anthem, "I didn't do it! Nobody saw me do it! You can't prove anything." We chose not to let the White House once again become Bill's love nest. We refused to let the George Soros puppet in heels moves into the Oval Office with her rolodex of contributors both foreign and domestic.

So what do we have now? The Cartel and the politicians that follow them around like a children's pull toy on a string are screeching day and night the Russians! The Russians! They have Comey's BFF installed as the Special Counsel because of Comey's leaks. The stage is set for a sequel to the

Drain the Swamp

Progressives favorite thriller, "The Witch Hunt of Watergate."

What's a freedom loving constitutionalist to do? How about every time the Progressives issue a subpoena for one of the President's followers we issue one for a Debbie Wasserman Schultz, or her Pakistani IT money launderer, or Bill Clinton, or Loretta Lynch, or any of the shady characters who actually tried to fix the election. How about a Special Counsel to investigate all the scandals of the Obummer nightmare, Fast and Furious, Benghazi, Lois Lerner and the IRS, or the serial unmasking of American citizens for political purposes?

Why should we just roll over and take it? Why not take it and roll on instead? We won let's act like it!

If we don't stand up after the Miracle in November and demand that the swamp is drained when will it happen? When Crazy Bernie, Creepy Joe, Chelsea, AOC, or some other socialist gets elected? If we can't drain the swamp now the swamp is going to drain us right into the sewer of history.

Drain the Swamp

Dispatch Thirty-five

Common Threads in Mass Murders

As I contemplate the horror in Las Vegas I
wonder; is it only tragedy that unites us.
Or is it a tragedy that we are divided.

I also wonder why does an important
common thread always seems to be missing
from every story examining the reasons for
these evil acts?

What is that common thread? Is it a
political affiliation? Is it a nationality? Is it
a certain type of weapon? No. None of
these is the common thread.

Overwhelming evidence points to the signal
largest common factor in all of these
incidents is the fact that all of the
perpetrators were either actively taking
powerful psychotropic drugs or had been at
some point in the immediate past before
they committed their crimes.

It is the use of psychotropic drugs such as antidepressants that ties so many of these horrific events together. In case after case the perpetrators were either taking them or they had been taking them recently. Anyone who has ever tried to kick a drug habbit knows the depths of depression that can bring.

According to the Citizens Commission on Human Rights International, "At least 36 school shootings and/or school-related acts of violence have been committed by those taking or withdrawing from psychiatric drugs resulting in 172 wounded and 80 killed (in other school shootings, information about their drug use was never made public—neither confirming or refuting if they were under the influence of prescribed drugs)."[241]

---

[241] *Plain Truth*, 5-22-18, accessed 6-21-19 https://www.plaintruth.com/the_plain_truth/2018/05/school-shootings-mental-health-watchdog-says-psychotropic-drug-use-by-school-shooters-merits-federal-investigation.html

Drain the Swamp

Dan Roberts of AmmoLand has compiled the following partial list:[242]

Eric Harris age 17 (first on Zoloft then Luvox) and Dylan Klebold aged 18 (Columbine school shooting in Littleton, Colorado), killed 12 students and 1 teacher, and wounded 23 others, before killing themselves. Klebold's medical records have never been made available to the public.

• Jeff Weise, age 16, had been prescribed 60 mg/day of Prozac (three times the average starting dose for adults!) when he shot his grandfather, his grandfather's girlfriend and many fellow students at Red Lake, Minnesota. He then shot himself. 10 dead, 12 wounded.

• Cory Baadsgaard, age 16, Wahluke (Washington state) High School, was on Paxil (which caused him to have hallucinations) when he took a rifle to his high school and held 23 classmates

---

[242] Roberts, D., Ammoland, 4-1-13, accessed 6-21-19 https://www.ammoland.com/2013/04/every-mass-shooting-in-the-last-20-years-shares-psychotropic-drugs/#axzz5rTrIK4ER

hostage. He has no memory of the event.

- Chris Fetters, age 13, killed his favorite aunt while taking Prozac.

- Christopher Pittman, age 12, murdered both his grandparents while taking Zoloft.

- Mathew Miller, age 13, hung himself in his bedroom closet after taking Zoloft for 6 days.

- Kip Kinkel, age 15, (on Prozac and Ritalin) shot his parents while they slept then went to school and opened fire killing 2 classmates and injuring 22 shortly after beginning Prozac treatment.

- Luke Woodham, age 16 (Prozac) killed his mother and then killed two students, wounding six others.

- A boy in Pocatello, ID (Zoloft) in 1998 had a Zoloft-induced seizure that caused an armed stand off at his school.

- Michael Carneal (Ritalin), age 14, opened fire on students at a high school prayer meeting in West Paducah, Kentucky. Three teenagers were killed, five others were wounded..

• A young man in Huntsville, Alabama (Ritalin) went psychotic chopping up his parents with an ax and also killing one sibling and almost murdering another.

• Andrew Golden, age 11, (Ritalin) and Mitchell Johnson, aged 14, (Ritalin) shot 15 people, killing four students, one teacher, and wounding 10 others.

• TJ Solomon, age 15, (Ritalin) high school student in Conyers, Georgia opened fire on and wounded six of his class mates.

• Rod Mathews, age 14, (Ritalin) beat a classmate to death with a bat.

• James Wilson, age 19, (various psychiatric drugs) from Breenwood, South Carolina, took a .22 caliber revolver into an elementary school killing two young girls, and wounding seven other children and two teachers.

Drain the Swamp

• Elizabeth Bush, age 13, (Paxil) was responsible for a school shooting in Pennsylvania

• Jason Hoffman (Effexor and Celexa) – school shooting in El Cajon, California

• Jarred Viktor, age 15, (Paxil), after five days on Paxil he stabbed his grandmother 61 times.

• Chris Shanahan, age 15 (Paxil) in Rigby, ID who out of the blue killed a woman.

• Jeff Franklin (Prozac and Ritalin), Huntsville, AL, killed his parents as they came home from work using a sledge hammer, hatchet, butcher knife and mechanic's file, then attacked his younger brothers and sister.

• Neal Furrow (Prozac) in LA Jewish school shooting reported to have been court-ordered to be on Prozac along with several other medications.

• Kevin Rider, age 14, was withdrawing from Prozac when he died from a gunshot wound to his head. Initially it was ruled a suicide, but two years later, the investigation into his death was opened as a possible homicide. The prime suspect, also age 14, had been taking Zoloft and other SSRI antidepressants.

• Alex Kim, age 13, hung himself shortly after his Lexapro prescription had been doubled.

• Diane Routhier was prescribed Welbutrin for gallstone problems. Six days later, after suffering many adverse effects of the drug, she shot herself.

• Billy Willkomm, an accomplished wrestler and a University of Florida student, was prescribed Prozac at the age of 17. His family found him dead of suicide – hanging from a tall ladder at the family's Gulf Shore Boulevard home in July 2002.

• Kara Jaye Anne Fuller-Otter, age 12, was on Paxil when she hung herself from a hook in her closet. Kara's parents said ".... the damn doctor wouldn't take her off it and I asked him to when we went in on the second visit. I told him I thought she was having some sort of reaction to Paxil...")

• Gareth Christian, Vancouver, age 18, was on Paxil when he committed suicide in 2002, (Gareth's father could not accept his son's death and killed himself.)

• Julie Woodward, age 17, was on Zoloft when she hung herself in her family's detached garage.

• Matthew Miller was 13 when he saw a psychiatrist because he was having difficulty at school. The psychiatrist gave him samples of Zoloft. Seven days later his mother found him dead, hanging by a belt from a laundry hook in his closet.

• Kurt Danysh, age 18, and on Prozac, killed his father with a shotgun. He is now behind prison bars, and writes letters, trying to warn the world that SSRI drugs can kill.

• Woody ___, age 37, committed suicide while in his 5th week of taking Zoloft. Shortly before his death his physician suggested doubling the dose of the drug. He had seen his physician only for insomnia. He had never been depressed, nor did he have any history of any mental illness symptoms.

• A boy from Houston, age 10, shot and killed his father after his Prozac dosage was increased.

• Hammad Memon, age 15, shot and killed a fellow middle school student. He had been diagnosed with ADHD and depression and was taking Zoloft and "other drugs for the conditions."

• Matti Saari, a 22-year-old culinary student, shot and killed 9 students and a teacher, and wounded another student, before killing himself. Saari was taking an SSRI and a benzodiazapine.

• Steven Kazmierczak, age 27, shot and killed five people and wounded 21 others before killing himself in a Northern Illinois University auditorium. According to his girlfriend, he had recently been taking Prozac, Xanax and Ambien. Toxicology results showed that he still had trace amounts of Xanax in his system.

• Finnish gunman Pekka-Eric Auvinen, age 18, had been taking antidepressants before he killed eight people and wounded a dozen more at Jokela High School – then he committed suicide.

• Asa Coon from Cleveland, age 14, shot and wounded four before taking his own life. Court records show Coon was on Trazodone.

• Jon Romano, age 16, on medication for depression, fired a shotgun at a teacher in his New York high school.

Why is this common thread being hidden by the Corporations Once Known as the Mainstream Media? Is it because of their anti-gun narrative? When they tell us about how many deaths by gun in America there are why don't they mention that the over 60% of those are suicides?[243]

---

[243] Sanger-Katz, M., *The New York Times*, 10-8-15, accessed 6-21-19
https://www.nytimes.com/2015/10/09/upshot/gun-deaths-are-mostly-suicides.html

The horror of this past week makes us all struggle to find a reason. No matter what the reason, no matter what drove this person to do this terrible thing I agree with the President when he said this was an act of pure evil.[244]

Another question this brings to mind: I find it interesting that in twelve hours the FBI can definitively tell us the person who perpetrated the horror had no ties to ISIS yet after a year of investigation turning up no evidence they can't tell whether or not President Trump colluded with the Russians to give Hillary a popular vote victory.

---

[244] Liptak, K., *The New York Times*, 10-2-17, accessed 6-21-19
https://www.cnn.com/2017/10/02/politics/donald-trump-las-vegas-shooting-remarks/index.html

Dispatch Thirty-six

Divided We Fall

United we stand has long been part of the inner strength that enabled America to rise from thirteen disjointed colonies on the edge of lonely sea to the pinnacle of power.

Some people believe in the Six Degrees of Separation Theory.[245] According to the theory everyone in the world are six or fewer steps away from each other and that a direct line such as "a friend of a friend" can be drawn to connect any two people in a maximum of six steps. Some people believe all of us are in this thing together, and that diversity is our strength and I am

---

[245] Top Documentary Films, 2009, accessed 6-21-19 https://topdocumentaryfilms.com/six-degrees-of-separation/

he as you are she as you are me and we are all together.[246]

Even if we're all connected in ways we cannot know I believe the world is filled with strangers. Take a ride and as you pass through country, town, and city you're constantly presented with the faces of people you'll never know, all of whom have lives and families that will never know you or your life or your family. Every day we see people we've never seen before and will never see again. They rise out of the mist beyond the pale of our personal knowledge and are immediately submerged again never to rise again. Our only and forever our only connection will be that one fleeting moment when we moved through a single frame of the separate sagas of our lives.

Unlike Cain I do believe we're our brother's keeper, and unlike Scrooge I believe we should help our brothers in need instead of seeing them boiled in their own pudding and buried with a stake of holly through their hearts. However, unlike the rhetoric of

---

[246] Letras, accessed 6-21-19
https://www.letras.com/the-beatles/184/

Marx, Lenin, and ex-President Obama I don't believe that life should operate on the basis of from each according to their ability to each according to their need,[247] or as we say in America today, spreading the wealth around.[248]

In other words, I'm not a socialist. I believe in personal liberty, individual freedom, and economic opportunity. I found myself out of phase with the Progressive Clique which successfully maneuvered its way to power using the education system, the media, and until 2016 uninformed, uninvolved, and emotional voters.

Out of phase or not, I believe in the equality of opportunity which gives everyone a shot at success as opposed to the equality of outcome which the Progressives and their fellow travelers wish to foist upon us, which gives everyone the assurance of mediocrity. No matter the consequence, no matter the sacrifice we must stand up for what we

---

[247] Marx, K., Brainyquotes, accessed 6-21-19 https://www.brainyquote.com/quotes/karl_marx_13 6396
[248] Youtube, https://www.youtube.com/watch?v=OoqI5PSRcXM

believe or we'll stand by while our nation is transformed into what we won't be able to believe is still called the United States of America.[249]

Day by day the bean counting pencil pushers, who make up the nameless faceless bureaucracy that is the Deep State, grind out rule after rule and regulation after regulation. President Obama's signature piece of legislation, Obamacare churned out thousands upon thousands of pages of federal requirements all meant to fill in the blanks in a 2600 page bill that we had to pass to find out what was in it.[250]

Hope and change became bait and switch. In 2012 Mr. Obama wasn't even trying to win votes from those who disagreed with him. He wasn't trying to change minds. He was trying to buy votes. He bet that generations of entitlements had finally

---

[249] Youtube, accessed 6-21-19
https://www.youtube.com/watch?v=KrefKCaV8m4
[250] Benson, G., Townhall, 3-12-13, accessed 6-21-19
https://townhall.com/tipsheet/guybenson/2013/03/1
2/photo-20000-pages-of-obamacare-regulations-
n1532069

birthed the lumpen proletariat[251] that his theories of government proclaim must exist for History to reach its summit. He bet his second term on the belief that there were enough people dependent upon the government that they would vote for a handout instead of voting for a hand up. He bet that America had been dumbed down enough and bribed enough to trade our heritage of freedom for the yoke of a guaranteed something instead of the opportunity for everything.

Class warfare, penalizing success, dividing America into interest groups and voter blocks this was the strategy Mr. Obama thought would win as he worked to build a coalition of leftist intellectuals, government insider and those convinced they were disenfranchised.[252] Looking at the polls it appeared he had the solid core of 40+%

---

[251] Encyclopedia of Marxism, accessed 6-21-19
https://www.marxists.org/glossary/terms/l/u.htm
[252] Edsall, T. *The New York Times*, 11-27-11, accessed 6-21-19
https://campaignstops.blogs.nytimes.com/2011/11/27/the-future-of-the-obama-coalition/?mtrref=undefined&gwh=73C26848D2C430285096EF059291FE5E&gwt=pay

who will vote for a Democrat even if he is the devil himself. The question was would the unengaged and uninformed voters who could at least hope he would change combined with the illegals and the dead who at least get to vote in Chicago be enough for him to win?

Of course it didn't hurt that the Republicans nominated a stiff who threw in the towel after winning the first debate.

Remember what a second Obama term looked like?

He won on the basis of a promise to double down on social democracy,[253] a complete disregard for the checks and balances meant to maintain the balance of power between the branches of government, and a desire to totally transform America.[254]

---

[253] The Free Dictionary, accessed 6-21-19
https://www.thefreedictionary.com/social+democrac
y
[254] Brownfield, M., *The Daily Signal*, 12-11-11, accessed 6-21-19
https://www.dailysignal.com/2011/12/14/constitutio
n-anyone-obama-promises-to-rule-without-
congress/

Drain the Swamp

After the last four years of the Obamanation when he ruled by one unconstitutional decree after another and no one opposed anything he did what is left of the America we've known? How will we ever get back to where we came from? No entitlement once enacted has ever been repealed. The size of government never shrinks. The power it usurps from the people and the States is never surrendered.

What's a constitutional libertarian independent to do?

A world filled with strangers keeps getting stranger all the time. No matter how many degrees of separation actually exist we should never be as divided as the Progressives and their identity politics try to portray us. We're Americans. We can do better than this. Reject the siren song of free entitlements which are never free, and embrace the liberty our forefathers won for us. Let's renew the great experiment in human freedom and strive to see our nation rise again as the last best hope of man that it was meant to be. The shining city on a hill that can light the way to a future worthy of free men and women held together by unity not disjointed in our separation.

Even if it takes more than six degrees of separation to connect to others what does it matter how connected we are to people around the world if we are in terminal disagreement with our fellow Americans? As a nation we're divided between those who want to strive to achieve and those who thrive because they receive. The Progressives have bred generations of passive takers who believe they're entitled to the fruit of others' labor. They pay no taxes so they don't care how high taxes go. They have no conception of paying for what they have, so they don't care about the national debt. They see America as a vending machine, so they don't believe in our unique place in History. They desire a shabby world of bread and circuses based on equality of outcome, so they don't long to be all they can be.

Those of us who want America to be what America has been and what it should be, the home of the brave and the land of the free can't let divisions divide us anymore!

We must unite to save liberty or we will stand alone at the end of the day. We may be strangers to one another. We may not know each other but if we're fellow believers in personal liberty, individual freedom, and economic opportunity we must unite over what connects us to save what has always made us E PLURIBUS UNUM.[255]

A final thought: Just as we have prospered as no nation before through the application of "United we stand" so too will we reap the results of its mirror image: "Divided we fall."

---

[255] The Great Seal, accessed 6-21-19
http://www.greatseal.com/mottoes/unum.html

Drain the Swamp

Dispatch Thirty-seven

AntiFa Terrorists in League with ISIS and Al Qaeda

The violent left wing revolutionaries who identify themselves as AntiFa[256] are announcing[257] to the world that they plan[258] on staging a major attack[259] on American democracy beginning Saturday November 4th.

---

[256] Tuttle, I., *National Review*, 6-5-17, accessed 6-21-19
https://www.nationalreview.com/2017/06/antifa-protest-donald-trump-roots-left-wing-political-violence/
[257] Refuse Fascism, 8-6-17, accessed 6-21-19
https://refusefascism.org/2017/08/06/this-nightmare-must-end-the-trumppence-regime-must-go/
[258] *World Net Daily*, 10-1-17, accessed 6-21-19
https://www.wnd.com/2017/10/antifa-mass-uprising-to-remove-fascist-trump/
[259] *World Net Daily*, 10-27-17, accessed 6-21-19
https://www.wnd.com/2017/10/communist-front-group-behind-uprising-planned-nov-4/

Drain the Swamp

These brutish thugs have attempted to terrorize the American people since last year's presidential campaign. They staged violent protests at many Trump campaign events. In Chicago one event had to be cancelled[260] because the police could not guarantee Mr. Trump's safety. If you noticed none of Hillary's campaign events were attacked by the supporters of Mr. Trump or the AntiFa bully boys.

At their philosophical home, Berkeley they routinely strive to deny free speech using violence and confrontation to silence anyone who disagrees[261] with their collectivist vision of Amerika. Spreading in concentric circles of hate the AntiFa[262] thugs routinely

---

[260] Elliott, P., *Time*, 3-12-16, accessed 6-21-17 https://time.com/4256529/donald-trump-chicago-rally-protest-cancel/
[261] Parzar, J., *The Los Angeles Times*, 9-15-17, accessed 6-21-19 https://www.latimes.com/local/california/la-me-berkeley-protest-shapiro-20170914-htmlstory.html
[262] *World Net Daily*, 1-21-18, accessed 6-21-19 https://www.wnd.com/2018/01/antifa-revealed-free-expose-of-alt-left/

302

attempt to squash free speech[263] on campuses across the country.

Now damning new evidence is being presented by veteran newsman Edward Klein, who is the former editor in chief of the New York Times Magazine in his new book, *All Out War: The Plot to Destroy Trump*.

In this book Mr. Klein presents convincing evidence that the AntiFa domestic terrorists have held meeting with representatives of both ISIS and Al Qaeda. He also reveals that members of the leftwing hate group have traveled to Syria for training.

The author quotes an FBI report that stated, "There is clearly overwhelming evidence that there are growing ties between U.S. radicals and the Islamic State, as well as several [ISIS] offshoots and splinter groups."

During last year's G-20 meetings in Hamburg, Germany the many of the AntiFa

---

[263] *World Net Daily*, 10-30-17, accessed 6-21-19 https://www.wnd.com/2017/10/antifa-now-threatens-free-speech-on-campus/

brigands staged pre-planned riots protesting President Trump and railing against capitalism. Numerous police officers were injured and property was destroyed.[264] At least one elected Democrat official, Mayor Bill De Blasio of New York whose expenses were paid by the organizers of the protests,[265] flew over and participated.[266]

The FBI report continued, "(The) Task force covered G20 meeting in Hamburg, studied intel from local authorities, Interpol, and other assets, determined that as assumed U.S.-backed anarchist/radical groups had traveled to Germany and took place in the violence ... There is also evidence of meetings between these individuals and associates of ISIS. There is an urgent need to closely surveil the identified individuals."

---

[264] Sexton, J., 7-6-17, *Hotair*, 7-6-17, accessed 6-21-19 https://hotair.com/archives/2017/07/06/anti-capitalists-protest-g20-summit-germany-seven-police-officers-injured/
[265] Calder, R., *New York Post*, 7-7-17, accessed 6-21-19 https://nypost.com/2017/07/07/de-blasio-begins-all-expense-paid-trip-to-g20-protests/
[266]*The New York Times*, accessed 6-21-19 https://www.nytimes.com/2017/07/06/nyregion/de-blasio-makes-sudden-trip-to-trump-protests-at-g-20-summit.html

The FBI report is chilling. It outlines the growth of a cancer on the body politic of our Republic not seen since the heyday of the KKK, another organization linked to the Democrat Party.[267]

Here are some more statements from the report as chronicled by the Daily Mail.com:[268]

"Now that the bureau has determined they have followers in the radical U.S. resistance movement in the United States, it is clear there will be additional violence in the attacks on law enforcement and U.S. institutions, including banks."

"Ties between three key leaders of the Oakland group [names redacted] met in Hamburg with a leader of the AQAP [Al Qaeda in the Arabian Peninsula] and the AQIM [Al Qaeda in the Islamic Maghreb],' the report continued. 'The leader from AQAP is an Egyptian-born male [name redacted]

---

[267] *World Net Daily*, 10-25-17, accessed 6-21-19
https://www.wnd.com/2007/10/44171/
[268] Klein, E., *Daily Mail*, 10-29-17, accessed 6-21-19
https://www.wnd.com/2007/10/44171/

who is known to be in charge of finances and recruiting for the group."

"There is evidence from informants that he is helping the Oakland group acquire the weapons they are seeking, primarily bomb making equipment and toxic chemicals and gasses."

"One of the men from Oakland traveled to Syria to meet with ISIS; the purpose was for training in tactics, but was thought to be primarily a bonding visit to discuss possible massive disruptive attacks in the U.S."

"While in Hamburg, several of the Oakland-based criminals were photographed throwing Molotov cocktails and wielding iron bars, which have been their weapons of choice, though they are almost certainly on the verge of upping the caliber of their weaponry for use in the U.S."

"Despite having their faces covered by masks, they were positively identified."

"This group and their connections with the radical Islamic groups must be disrupted and destroyed."

The FBI field report was delivered to Acting Director Andrew McCabe in July.

According to a source quoted by the Daily Mail, "The FBI is really playing catchup ball, because the Obama administration refused to give the bureau the resources it needed to effectively infiltrate and surveil the radical groups on college campuses,"[269] the source continued. ...

"Any talk of a connection between radical Islam—a phrase the Obama people wouldn't even use—and American extremists was pretty much laughed off. [Former Attorney General] Loretta Lynch would have blown a gasket if she heard that the FBI was surveilling so-called college political organizations. ..."[270]

"All that has changed under the Trump administration. Everyone's aware that the resistance movement, with its effort to get rid of Trump by any means necessary, has

---

[269] Ibid.
[270] Ibid.

created fertile soil for ISIS and al Qaeda to establish a beachhead in America."[271]

The growth and anti-American nature of the AntiFa movement is aided, abetted, and covered up by the Corporations Once Known As the Mainstream Media.[272]

Many Democrat voters in America have no idea that these elements of their party are entering into treasonous relationships with America's enemies during a time of war. They have no idea that their votes which prop-up the reigns of perpetually re-elected hacks such as Nancy Pelosi, Chuck Schumer, and Maxine Waters encourages and supports the Resist 45 Movement which is the cover for these domestic terrorists.[273]

They have no idea though the information is readily available with just the click of a mouse. They have no idea that the AntiFa

---

[271] Ibid.

[272] *World Net Daily*, 10-14-17, accessed 6-21-19 https://www.wnd.com/2017/10/media-cover-up-of-antifa-antics/

[273] Holland, J., *The Nation*, 2-6-17, accessed 6-21-19 https://www.thenation.com/article/your-guide-to-the-sprawling-new-anti-trump-resistance-movement/

Blackshirts and their hate depend upon the support of useful idiots[274] to give them the rope they will use to hang them.[275]

Turn the game off and tune in. Your country is being set up for a revolution. Don't let a vocal violent minority working with foreign enemies pull the wool over your eyes. If they were the legitimate loyal opposition they wouldn't be wearing ski masks and conspiring with ISIS and Al Qaeda to over throw the President of the United States.

---

[274] Lexico, accessed 6-21-19
https://www.lexico.com/en/definition/useful_idiot
[275] Lenin, V., Liberty Tree, accessed 6-21-19
http://libertytree.ca/quotes/Vladimir.Lenin.Quote.06 8C

Dispatch Thirty-eight

Hillary and the DNC Front Group

In the run-up to the 2016 presidential election and during the ensuing campaign the Democratic National Committee acted as a front group for the Hillary campaign. If not breaking laws certainly trampling on the spirit of the law in its unbridled pursuit of power.

The DNC sold its soul to the Hillary campaign. Donna Brazile was the interim head of the DNC during and right after the election. She took over after the artful dodger, Debbie Wasserman Schultz who had been run out of Dodge after leaked emails should the depth of her complicity in the rigged primary.[276] According to Ms.

---

[276] Seitz-Wald, A., NBC, 7-24-16, accessed 6-21-19 https://www.nbcnews.com/storyline/2016-conventions/democratic-national-committee-chief-stepping-aside-after-convention-n615826

Brazile, "Debbie was not a good manager. She hadn't been very interested in controlling the party—she let Clinton's headquarters in Brooklyn do as it desired. ..."

Brazille wanted to explain to Bernie Sanders whether or not the leaked emails which had brought down the former Chair concerning the way Hillary had rigged the primary were true.

It took her months to ferret out the truth from DNC staffers and former Hillary campaign operatives all working overtime to keep their previous plots and plans from seeing the light of day.

Hillary said, "the party from the ground up ... when our state parties are strong, we win. That's what will happen."[277]

In reality the states kept less than half of 1 percent of the $82 million they had

---

[277] Brazile, D., *Politico Magazine*, 11-2-17, accessed 6-21-19
https://www.politico.com/magazine/story/2017/11/0 2/clinton-brazile-hacks-2016-215774

amassed from the extravagant fund-raisers Hillary's campaign was holding.[278]

Politico described this arrangement as "essentially ... money laundering"[279] for the Clinton campaign while Hillary hypocritically made campaign finance reform part of her platform.

After months of stonewalling by Hillary's former campaign people and their fellow travelers in the DNC Barzile found an "agreement—signed by Amy Dacey, the former CEO of the DNC, and Robby Mook with a copy to Marc Elias—specified that in exchange for raising money and investing in the DNC, Hillary would control the party's finances, strategy, and all the money raised. Her campaign had the right of refusal of who would be the party communications director, and it would make final decisions on all the other staff. The DNC also was required to consult with the campaign about all other staffing, budgeting, data, analytics, and mailings."[280]

---

[278] Ibid.
[279] Ibid.
[280] Ibid.

Drain the Swamp

Here's how Barzile explained the unusual nature of Hillary's control of the DNC, "When the party chooses the nominee, the custom is that the candidate's team starts to exercise more control over the party. If the party has an incumbent candidate, as was the case with Clinton in 1996 or Obama in 2012, this kind of arrangement is seamless because the party already is under the control of the president. When you have an open contest without an incumbent and competitive primaries, the party comes under the candidate's control only after the nominee is certain. When I was manager of Gore's campaign in 2000, we started inserting our people into the DNC in June. This victory fund agreement, however, had been signed in August 2015, just four months after Hillary announced her candidacy and nearly a year before she officially had the nomination."

That's right only four months after she declared her candidacy Hillary took effective control of the DNC. Bernie never had a chance and all the insiders knew it from the beginning. Before the Wikileaks email dump Bernie was ignorant of this though he continually said that the system was rigged.[281] He even predicted a contested convention. How that must have brought smiles to the faces of the backroom hacks running the Democrat slight-of-hand. After it was revealed Bernie endorsed Hillary,[282] tried to bring the Sandernistas with him, and campaigned vigorously for a woman he knew to be totally corrupt.[283]

All of this evidence of Hillary's campaign irregularities has been exposed by Donna Brazile a long-time Democrat operative and one-time faux journalist on the Clinton News Network. Remember she was with CNN she funneled the questions to Hillary

[281] Schwartz, I., *Real Clear Politics*, 5-2-16, accessed 6-21-19
https://www.realclearpolitics.com/video/2016/05/02/sanders_there_will_be_a_contested_convention_system_is_rigged.html
[282] Lee, M. & J. Zeleny, CNN, 7-12-16, accessed 6-21-19
https://www.realclearpolitics.com/video/2016/05/02/sanders_there_will_be_a_contested_convention_system_is_rigged.html
[283] Meckler, L., *The Wall Street Journal*, 10-8-16, accessed 6-21-19
https://www.wsj.com/articles/bernie-sanders-packs-schedule-with-campaign-stops-for-hillary-clinton-1475928002

before the debate. The rats are leaving the ship indeed.[284]

As the cover is pulled off the cover-up one of the strange things about this expose' is that Seth Rich, a DNC staffer who was killed in Washington, D.C. last year was one of the people listed in the dedication to Ms. Brazile's book.[285] And how she describes her reaction to Mr. Rich's untimely death is another interesting view into the operations of what may well be described as a criminal enterprise disguised as a political party. Brazile writes that after Rich's unsolved murder, she feared for her life, shutting blinds so snipers could not see her, and placing surveillance cameras inside her home.[286]

---

[284] Scarry, E., *The Washington Examiner*, 3-17-17, accessed 6-21-19
https://www.washingtonexaminer.com/donna-brazile-finally-admits-she-shared-debate-questions-with-clinton-campaign
[285] CBS, 7-12-19, accessed 6-21-19
https://www.cbsnews.com/news/seth-rich-shot-democratic-national-committee-staffer-washington-dc/
[286] Watson, K., CBS, 11-4-17, accessed 6-21-19

And from the Surprise-Surprise-Surprise Department, "Network newscasts don't mention Brazile Clinton-DNC revelations."[287]

I have to echo President Trump on this one, "Everybody is asking why the Justice Department (and FBI) isn't looking into all of the dishonesty going on with Crooked Hillary & the Dems."[288] Which was followed by another comment I believe most of us would agree with, "At some point the Justice Department, and the FBI, must do what is right and proper. The American public deserves it!"[289]

That's right. We deserve to know the truth and we can't depend on the exclusively on the ABCCBSNBCCNNMSNBCNPRPBS Cartel to get the news out. We need to do it ourselves. Tell everyone you know, tweet

[287] Concha, J., *The Hill*, 11-3-17, accesed 6-21-19 https://thehill.com/homenews/media/358589-network-newscasts-dont-mention-brazile-clinton-dnc-revelations
[288] Jenkins, N., *Time*, 11-3-17, accessed 6-21-19 https://time.com/5008708/donald-trump-twitter-hillary-clinton-dnc/
[289] Nelson, L., *Politico*, 1-3-17, accessed 6-21-19 https://www.politico.com/story/2017/11/03/trump-doj-investigate-hillary-clinton-244505

it, post it, re-post spread the word far and near.   Hillary and New York's Sixth Crime Family are the ones who have attempted to subvert our republic for their personal gain. And now they are trying to reverse the results of last year's election through a silent coup.

Stand up for what's right.   Or you'll fall for what's wrong.

Drain the Swamp

Dispatch Thirty-nine

A Protection Racket Wrapped in a Cover-up

Is the entire Mueller investigation a false flag distraction to cover the tracks of the people who really did attempt to undermine an American presidential election?

Some background to this part of the plot must include the fact that the former FBI Director James Comey has admitted to illegally leaking transcripts of privileged conversations with the President to the press. Why did he do it? Comey testified before a Senate Committee that he orchestrated the leak of accounts of conversations with President Donald Trump because he thought it might lead to the appointment of a special prosecutor to lead the Russia investigation.[290]

In an interesting twist Deputy Attorney General, Rod J. Rosenstein in a memo to the President on May 9, 2017 after outlining the improper actions of James Comey with regard to the investigation of Hillary's emails stated, "Although the President has the power to remove an FBI director, the decision should not be taken lightly. I agree with the nearly unanimous opinions of former Department officials. The way the Director handled the conclusion of the email investigation was wrong. As a result, the FBI is unlikely to regain public and congressional trust until it has a Director who understands the gravity of the mistakes and pledges never to repeat them. Having refused to admit his errors, the Director cannot be expected to implement the necessary corrective actions."[291]

---

[290] Collinson, S., CNN, 6-8-17, accessed 6-21-18 https://www.cnn.com/2017/06/08/politics/james-comey-testimony-donald-trump/index.html
[291] BBC, 5-10-17, accessed 6-21-19 https://www.bbc.com/news/world-us-canada-39866767

Accepting this counsel President Trump fired FBI Director Comey. Then Deputy Attorney General, Rod J. Rosenstein appointed Mueller as Special Counsel to investigate Trump based on his firing of Comey.

President Trump knows what's going on. In his famous tweet where he labeled Mueller's fishing expedition a "Witch Hunt" he said "I am being investigated for firing the FBI Director by the man who told me to fire the FBI Director!"[292]

Mueller, who is up to his eyeballs in Hillary's Russian scams, has weaponized criminal law in the convoluted attempt of the Progressive cult to misdirect the public.[293] The denizens of the swamp never expected Hillary to lose. They never thought there was any chance of their nefarious and perhaps treasonous schemes to stack the deck and short circuit the electoral processes. But in

---

[292] Lizza, R., *The New Yorker*, 6-16-17, accessed 6-21-19 https://www.newyorker.com/news/ryan-lizza/why-trump-attacked-his-own-deputy-attorney-general

[293] Hart, R., *The Daily Caller*, 10-31-17, accessed 6-21-19 https://dailycaller.com/2017/10/31/mueller-is-weaponizing-criminal-law-for-political-gain/

a shocking twist the electoral system designed by our founders worked and the united people out here in fly-over country were able to thwart the bi-coastal fix when the fix was supposedly in.

The gators, mosquitos, and apes of the swamp couldn't abide this travesty. So, the impartial Justice Department stepped in to claw back the reins of power from the great unwashed masses attempting to stage a revolution through the ballot box. According to an analysis by *The Hill* of the fourteen major federal agencies whose employees personally donated to presidential politics "By the end of September 2016, about $1.9 million, or 95 percent, went to the Democratic nominee's campaign."[294] And an astounding ninety-four percent of DOJ employee donations were to Hillary. Nothing to see here no bias there move along.

So far Mueller and his team of democrat donors have secured the indictment of Paul

---

[294] Swan, J., *The Hill*, 10-26-16, accessed 6-21-19 https://thehill.com/homenews/campaign/302817-government-workers-shun-trump-give-big-money-to-clinton-campaign

Manafort whose main crime may have been working in the Trump campaign. Wait a minute how can you say that! He wasn't indicted for anything to do with Trump's campaign. No, he was indicted for tax fraud and lobbying violations. Of course with the twisted and murky tax code that stretches to 73,954 pages. Then again as the old saying concerning Grand Juries goes "Prosecutors could get them to indict a ham sandwich."

As in any over-regulated state everyone is guilty of something they just haven't decided to pick you up yet. Let's see if we give an ex-FBI chief an unlimited budget, a big Democrat donor staff, and our bewildering multitude of laws in America, they'll eventually get anyone they want to much like a policeman following you for 1,000 miles. Eventually he will find a reason to pull you over.

It isn't even just a question of is this fair? It comes down to a decision. Is this the type of legal system we want in America? Do we want to have the banana-republic type of kangaroo justice that indicts, arrests, and convicts people over their politics?

The information of Hillary and her minions in the State Department and the FBI regarding their lucrative dealings with Russia and their machinations to deprive Bernie of any chance to win the primaries spill out like garbage from a ruptured plastic bag. And all the while we have the spectacle of those implicated by real evidence directing an investigation that goes nowhere and proves nothing.

A protection racket wrapped in a cover-up is playing out every day in the screaming headlines and impassioned screeds of the on-air teleprompter readers of the Corporations Once Known as the Mainstream Media. The only real questions left are:

Will the establishment succeed in casting out the interloper?

Will they reverse the 2016 election and expose that we have devolved from a representative republic operating on democratic principles into a functioning oligarchy disguised as a non-functional democracy.

And there are two other questions that rattle around in my mind:

Who would Putin rather have as the president a totally corrupt political hack that everyone knows is for sale or a self-made billionaire that no one can bribe, whose energy mantra is "Drill Baby Drill" and whose platform is America First?

And if the Russians hacked the election and Hillary won the popular vote whose side were they on? Evidently even the smartest woman in the world didn't understand how the Electoral College works maybe the Russians didn't either?

Drain the Swamp

Dispatch Forty

Impeach Mueller!

IMPEACH TRUMP! IMPEACH TRUMP!
IMPEACH TRUMP!

That is the screech we're about to hear
emanating from the denizens of the
swamp. Sure Maxine Waters and a few
others have been singing this song since
election night when their plans for the last
nail in our coffin went down in flames. Now
it's beginning to percolate through the
monotone media megaphone. And though
this was predicted in this column by this
author before the inauguration it still has a
jarring impact on the senses.

Back in the Dream Times when the Deep
State was able to turn Watergate into a
silent coup the precedent was set. If
someone tries to overturn the
moneychanger's tables they must be

destroyed. If it's a president, even one elected for the sole purpose of adding some reality to the mirage of our functioning oligarchy which portrays itself as a dysfunctional democratic republic, they must be hounded out of office, disgraced, and discredited.

That's the play book. Since before the inauguration the perpetually re-elected hacks aided and abetted by the ABCCBSNBCCNNMSNBCPBS Cartel and their paleo partners in print latched on to their intended weapon, "The Russians are coming! The Russians are coming!"

No matter that the initial facts of the story are ludicrous: the fictional Golden Shower Dossier[295] and the Russian hack of the DNC, which was in fact an inside job.[296] It doesn't matter that the very foundation of the Russian collusion theory is built on sand. Al that matters is that they now have

---

[295] Gillespie, N., *reason*, 10-1-17, accessed 6-21-19 https://reason.com/2017/01/10/hey-heres-that-obviously-fake-dossier-cl
[296] *World Net Daily*, 5-15-17, accessed 6-21-19 https://www.wnd.com/2017/05/dead-dnc-staffer-had-contact-with-wikileaks/

a Special Counselor. They can't call him a Special Prosecutor because there's no legal foundation to appoint a Special Prosecutor, so if they call him a Special Counselor that should fool all of us out here in fly-over country.

Prosecutors always believe whoever they're investigating is guilty and that their job is to find enough evidence to prove what they believe. Innocent until you are proven guilty, right. Anyone who has ever been unlucky enough to have be involved in a criminal trial and lived to talk about it knows how that feels in reality. It has inspired some to look at the courthouse and say, "It may say justice on the outside but there isn't any on the inside."

Remember the Valerie Plame investigation? Someone blew her cover as an undercover CIA operative. Before the investigation even started they knew who did it. Eventually after a few years and millions of dollars they never prosecuted anyone for the leak; instead they prosecuted Lewis "Scooter" Libby the Chief of Staff of Vice President Dick Chaney for inconsistencies in his testimony, a process crime.[297]

These are search and destroy missions. They are looking to get as many convictions as they can to justify all of their expenses and to puff up the reputations of the scalp hunters who run them. This Special "Counselor" is one of the closest associates of James "The Leaker" Comey.[298] He is staffing his office with Obama and Hillary supporters and we're supposed to believe his investigation of a non-crime that never happened will produce objective results that anyone anywhere would imagine are justice?[299]

Witch hunts find witches. That's what they do.

---

[297] Herman, A., *Commentary*, 7-15, accessed 6-21-19
https://www.commentarymagazine.com/articles/the-smearing-of-scooter-libby/
[298] Jarrett, G., Fox News, 6-12-17, accessed
https://www.foxnews.com/opinion/gregg-jarrett-are-mueller-and-comey-colluding-against-trump-by-acting-as-co-special-counsel
[299] Jarrett, K., *Townhalll*, 6-13-17, accessed
https://townhall.com/tipsheet/katiepavlich/2017/06/13/hmmm-special-counsel-muellers-team-sure-is-stacked-with-democrat-donors-n2340655

Drain the Swamp

If anyone was interested in finding real collusion to disrupt an American election they could look into the subject of the DNC emails leaked to WikiLeaks; the proven collusion between the Hillary Clinton campaign and Debbie Wasserman Schultz as revealed by unindicted co-conspirator Donna Brazile.[300] Did you ever notice that none of the principles ever denied what was in the leaked emails, they merely complained about who leaked what to who. Why isn't there a Special Counsel looking in to how these people stacked the cards against poor old Bernie Sanders? He said all along the election was rigged and he was right after all.[301] Why no interest in this? It doesn't serve to keep the swamp damp that's why.

Our elite masters, the perpetually re-elected, the Deeps State, and the Media Cartel are setting the stage. They must

---

[300] Mercia, D. & Maegan Vazquez, CNN, 11-2-17, accessed https://www.cnn.com/2017/11/02/politics/donna-brazile-dnc-book/index.html

[301] *Real Clear Politics*, 11-7-17, accessed 6-21-19 https://www.realclearpolitics.com/2017/11/07/berni e_sanders_was_right_it_was_rigged_425854.html

drive Trump from office before he can actually drain the swamp. They must drive him out disgraced and repudiated or else the poor blind masses might figure out that we don't need technocrats to rule us. If a professional business man is necessary to clean up the mess professional politicians have made, what do we need professional politicians for?

Now it turns out that Special Counsel Robert Mueller kept secret that Peter Strzok[302] a top FBI investigator exchanged anti-Trump text messages with an FBI attorney.[303] This transparent bias fuels questions about Mueller's credibility and his ability to oversee an impartial investigation. It was revealed that Strzok helped push the largely unverified dossier on Trump,[304] oversaw both the Clinton email and Russia collusion

---

[302] *The Wall Street Journal*, 12-4-17, accessed https://www.wsj.com/articles/muellers-credibility-problem-1512432318
[303] Ross, C., *The Daily Caller*, 12-4-17, accessed https://dailycaller.com/2017/12/04/anti-trump-text-messages-show-pattern-of-bias-on-muellers-team/
[304] Browne, P., Fox News, 12-5-17, accessed 6-21-19 https://www.foxnews.com/politics/fired-fbi-official-at-center-of-flynn-clinton-dossier-controversies-revealed

investigations, and conducted the July 2, 2016 interview with Hillary Clinton as well as the interview with Flynn.[305] Several weeks later, he was handpicked to oversee the investigation into possible collusion between the Trump campaign and Russian government. Add all this to the fact that Mueller has packed his investigating team with Clinton Supporters and there you have it, a fair and unbiased effort by the Deep State to remove President Trump from office.[306]

They won't let little things like votes, or facts, or what's good for America get in their way. No, they'll soldier on and soon we'll hear their longed for victory chant "IMPEACH TRUMP!!!! IMPEACH TRUMP!!!!" echoing through the halls of Rome on the Potomac.

To which I say, "Impeach Mueller!"

---

[305] Ibid.

[306] Kirby, B., *Lifezette*, 6-12-17, accessed 6-21-19 https://www.lifezette.com/2017/06/robert-mueller-stocks-staff-democrat-donors/

Drain the Swamp

Dispatch Forty-one

The Smoking Gun

Let's see; the Clinton campaign pays for a former British spy to work with Russian intelligence to create a bogus document that is then used as the basis for wiretaps aimed at the Trump campaign and the media is trying to tell us, "Move along nothing to see here."

Was the so-called dossier a hit piece from the begging? Maybe we should listen to Mary Jacoby, the wife of Glenn Simpson, the former Wall Street Journal reporter who started Fusion GPS, the firm behind the dossier.

She said on Facebook, "It's come to my attention that some people still don't realize what Glenn's role was in exposing Putin's control of Donald Trump. Let's be clear. Glenn conducted the investigation. Glenn hired Chris Steele. Chris Steele worked for Glenn."[307]

According to the website *Tablet*, "In June, three months after being hired by the lawyers for the Clinton campaign and the DNC, Simpson brought on Steele—but Steele hadn't lived or worked in Russia in nearly 25 years. Since he was identified as a British spy in 1999, and was head of the Russia desk when Russian assassins killed FSB defector Alexander Litvinenko in a sushi restaurant in the British capital, Steele was hardly in a position to make discreet inquiries. Still, Simpson must have thought Steele's name at a minimum would be useful in marketing whatever his firm pulled together. Reportedly, Steele had a good relationship with the FBI, and journalists love spies who spill secrets."[308]

---

[307] Wong, K., *Breitbart*, 12-22-17, accessed 6-21-19 https://www.breitbart.com/politics/2017/12/22/fusion-gps-obama-administration-weaponized-trump-dossier/
[308] Smith, L., *Tablet*, 12-20-17, accessed 6-21-19 https://www.breitbart.com/politics/2017/12/22/fusion-gps-obama-administration-weaponized-trump-dossier/

Of course having all this bogus information to accuse Trump would do no good if their candidate was indicted before the election (or after) so of course the crimes of Hillary Clinton had to again be whitewashed.

Found under the heading, "Wink, wink, nudge, nudge."

According to Rep. Matt Gaetz (R-FL) a member of the House Judiciary Committee, "I can certainly say that my impression after these interviews is that there was extreme pro-Hillary Clinton bias that benefitted her in this investigation and that she received special treatment as a consequence of her candidacy for president. … And we have email evidence from Andrew McCabe indicating that Hillary Clinton was going to get an 'HQ Special,' a headquarters special. That meant that the normal processes of the Washington field office weren't followed and he had a special. And he had a very small group of people that had a pro-Hillary Clinton bias who had a direct role in changing that investigation from one that likely should have been criminal to one where she was able to walk."[309]

What should Trump do?

Roger Stone in *Stone Cold Truth* gives this advice, "The president must completely disempower and dismantle Robert S. Mueller's fraudulent rogue prosecution gang, which is merely an extension of a larger corruption of power that is unparalleled in our history."[310]

Specifically he advises that the president must use every resource at his disposal to prosecute the almost-seditious abuses of power by lawless Clinton-Obama FBI and NSA apparatchiks who:[311]

Politically weaponized the federal government's electronic intelligence

[309] Poor, J., *Breitbart*, 12-22-17, accessed 6-21-19 https://www.breitbart.com/clips/2017/12/23/gop-rep-gaetz-email-evidence-andrew-mccabe-indicating-hillary-clinton-going-get-hq-special/
[310] Stone, R., Lew Rockwell.com, 12-22-17, accessed 6-21-19 https://www.lewrockwell.com/2017/12/roger-stone/trump-should-prosecute-the-illegal-nsa-cia-cabal-and-put-mueller-in-jail/
[311] Ibid.

capabilities to spy on a presidential candidate and his campaign

Colluded with foreign and non-state intelligence agents to manufacture evidence used as false pretexts for securing FISA warrants that employed the national security laws of the United States to give illicit, illegal cover to this political espionage

Used the fruits of this political espionage activity to damage or otherwise hinder this candidate, once he had become president-elect and eventually President of the United States, through surreptitious releases of the criminally-procured information,

Fabricated and instigated false allegations about foreign state collusion implicating the president's election campaign and family members, and

Perpetuated this massive criminal fraud on the American people for nearly a full year by manipulating and abusing the investigatory and prosecutorial powers of the Department of Justice.

He further fleshes this out with the advice to, "The president must order his Attorney

General to appoint a special counsel to investigate the Obama-Clinton-Mueller-Rosenstein criminal collusion that enriched the Clinton-Democrat crime syndicate by 100s of millions of dollars and further embedded the power of the deep state operators who facilitated what may be the most brazen of self-serving criminal treasons in American history: the multi-billion-dollar Uranium One pay-to-play scam. This incredible scheme perpetrated by the criminal Clintons and their coterie of minions and fellow travelers, implicates top officials of our federal government...including and especially the U.S Department of Justice, including and especially Robert Mueller and Rod Rosenstein."[312]

According to Rep. Peter King (R-NY) on Fox News, "If there's any collusion issue here, to me, it's the FBI, it's the Clinton campaign, it's the Russians for that matter because it could be very likely that Russians were feeding Steele information to use

---

[312] Ibid.

against Donald Trump and it was fake information."[313]

And now the rats begin to abandon ship.

The Justice Department's inspector general is conducting a broad investigation into how the department and FBI have handled recent matters, including the Clinton investigation. Deputy FBI Director Andrew McCabe's activities have been under scrutiny by the inspector general.[314]

McCabe's tenure has become entangled in recent years in politically charged controversies, including the investigation into Democrat Hillary Clinton's use of private email when she was secretary of State, and the ongoing criminal probe into whether Trump or his associates colluded

---

[313] Baker, T., *Breitbart*, 12-14-17, accessed 6-21-19
https://www.breitbart.com/clips/2017/12/24/gop-rep-peter-king-theres-collusion-fbi-clinton-campaign-russia/
[314] *Newsmax*, 12-23-17, accessed 6-21-19
https://www.newsmax.com/newsfront/mccabe-fbi-retire/2017/12/23/id/833478/

with Russia to interfere in the 2016 election campaign.[315]

McCabe, 49, has served as the No. 2 official at the FBI since February 2016, and would leave some time after he becomes fully eligible for pension benefits in March. So once we are liable to pay him a hefty pension for the rest of his life he leaves. I wonder if any future convictions might interfere with the delivery of that fat pay check to the prison commissary?

How could any of this obviously trumped up attack have any chance of success?

Just remember impeachment is not a criminal proceeding, it's a political one. If the House decides to Impeach a president they can call anything they want a high crime or misdemeanor or just invent one.

As former assistant U.S. attorney Andrew McCarthy said, "For argument's sake, let's assume the worst: Trump knew ⌊General Michael⌋ Flynn had lied to the FBI (i.e., that Flynn had committed at least one felony), and he leaned on Comey to close the FBI's

---

[315] Ibid.

probe. Even with those assumptions, there is still no obstruction case. The FBI and the Justice Department are not a separate branch of government; they are subordinates of the president delegated to exercise his power, not their own."[316] Therefore as McCarthy says, "There is no real crime because of the incontestable power of Trump to fire former FBI Director James Comey."[317]

One anti-Trumper author, Jennifer Rubin recently summed up the situation perfectly in the Washington Post, "The president doesn't need to commit a crime to be impeached."[318]

Just the claim of obstruction of justice will be enough for the Democrats to act, even if, in a strictly legal sense, no crime actually occurred.

---

[316] *World Net Daily*, 12-25-17, accessed 6-21-19 https://www.wnd.com/2017/12/democrats-real-plan-to-impeach-trump-in-2019/
[317] Ibid.
[318] *The Washington Post*, accessed 6-21-19 https://www.washingtonpost.com/blogs/right-turn/wp/2017/12/06/the-president-doesnt-need-to-have-committed-a-crime-to-be-impeached/?utm_term=.da29ee858a94

Drain the Swamp

If the Mueller fishing expedition fails to find any evidence of a real crime by Trump, or if he claims there is evidence of a process-crime such as obstruction of justice, Democrats are likely to use the special counsel's report as their platform for the midterm elections.

Therefore it will be the midterm elections that decide Trump's fate.

It all comes down to a plot starting in the Obama White House to undermine our democracy.

As Lee Smith of Tablet puts it, "To date the investigation into the Fusion GPS-manufactured collusion scandal has focused largely on the firm itself, its allies in the press, as well as contacts in the Department of Justice and FBI. However, if a sitting president used the instruments of state, including the intelligence community, to disseminate and legitimize a piece of paid opposition research in order to first obtain warrants to spy on the other party's campaign, and then to de-legitimize the results of an election once the other party's candidate won, we're looking at a scandal that dwarfs Watergate—a story not about a bad man in the White House, but about the subversion of key security institutions that are charged with protecting core elements of our democratic process while operating largely in the shadows."[319]

This is the smoking gun. Yes there was collusion. Yes there was (and is) a plot to undermine our system. And yes all the evidence is beginning to point straight at Obama, Hillary, and Democrat controlled Deep State. It is time to drain the swamp before America drowns in the filthy waters of a media enhanced whirlpool.

---

[319] Smith, L., Tablet, 12-20-17, accessed 6-21-19 https://www.breitbart.com/politics/2017/12/22/fusio n-gps-obama-administration-weaponized-trump-dossier/

Dispatch Forty-two

The Smoking Gun II

Hillary and her crew get a pass for colluding to stack the deck against Bernie. No matter what the evidence revealed the FBI nomenclature predetermined that New York's sixth crime family was untouchable. Congressional insiders report they have uncovered new irregularities and contradictions inside the FBI's probe of Hillary Clinton's email server.[320]

Investigators say there is written evidence that the FBI found evidence that some laws were broken when the former secretary of State and her top aides transmitted classified information through her insecure private email server.[321]

---

[320] Solomon, J., *The Hill*, 1-2-18, accessed 6-21-19
[321] Ibid.

That evidence includes passages in FBI documents stating the "sheer volume" of classified information that flowed through Clinton's insecure emails was proof of criminality.[322]

According to Sean Moran in Breitbart, "Former FBI Director James Comey's original memo regarding former Secretary of State Hillary Clinton's private email server was edited by FBI staffers to remove five references suggesting Clinton engaged in activities that would suggest felony and misdemeanor charges, according to obtained copies of the original memo."[323]

Looking into this matter Senate Homeland and Government Affairs Committee by Chairman Ron Johnson (R-WI) states, "The edits to Director Comey's public statement, made months prior to the conclusion of the FBI's investigation of Secretary Clinton's conduct, had a significant impact on the FBI's public evaluation of the implications of

---

[322] Ibid.
[323] Moran, S., *Breitbart*, 1-4-18, accessed https://www.breitbart.com/politics/2018/01/04/com eys-original-hillary-clinton-email-memo-suggested-possible-felony-violations/

her actions. … This effort, seen in light of the personal animus toward then-candidate Trump by senior agents leading the Clinton investigation and their apparent desire to create an 'insurance policy' against Mr. Trump's election, raise profound questions about the FBI's role and possible interference in the 2016 presidential election."[324]

Was there a concerted effort to interfere in in the election of 2016? Yes there was. And the activities of those who sought to impose their handpicked candidate Hillary Clinton, the last nail in our coffin need to be brought to light.

According to Andrew C. McCarthy in National Review, "When you look at it hard, two conclusions are impossible to escape: First, at the height of the 2016 campaign, Obama intelligence officials anxiously adopted Christopher Steele's allegations of traitorous conduct by then-candidate Donald Trump rather than first subject his "dossier" to rigorous investigation — even though Steele himself admits that his "raw,"

---

[324] Ibid.

"unverified" reports might not be true. Second, at the same time the FBI was receiving Steele's reports — which were based on multiple-hearsay from anonymous Russian sources, and paid for by the Clinton campaign — Obama intelligence officials were briefing congressional leaders about them, thereby ensuring that they'd be publicized just six weeks before Election Day."[325]

This was a brazen attempt to weaponize Steele's raw unverified 'Intelligence' seeking to use it to sink Trump's campaign.

This so-called intelligence was bought and paid for by the Clinton campaign. It used unverified sources and introduced what is now believed to be deceptive stories from a foreign power perhaps designed to influence the election by spreading false stories about Trump. If there was any Russian influence in all of this it was the introduction of it by the Clinton campaign and their bogus intelligence.

---

[325] McCarthy, A., *National Review*, 1-9-18, accessed https://www.nationalreview.com/2018/01/christopher-steele-dossier-obama-administration-hillary-clinton-campaign-congress-fisa-court/

According to Scott Uehlinger, a retired CIA Station Chief and Naval Officer in Newsmax, "As we move into 2018, we are seeing a rapid unravelling of the infamous Fusion GPS-Christopher Steele 'dossier.' With this discredited report dies the false narrative that the Trump Administration was involved in collusion with the Russian government. It's about time — the Justice Department investigation into 'Russian collusion' was always the fruit of this poisoned tree.

What should be disconcerting to Americans is that this document ever saw the light of day; much less that it formed the centerpiece of an official USG investigation. The whole sad affair demonstrates how far the professionalism of our Justice Department and Intelligence service has fallen in the wake of the rampant politicization that was the hallmark of the Obama Administration. "[326]

Add to this the team of anti-Trump ideologues assembled by Prosecutor-in-

---

Chief Mueller and the whole process is rotten from day one. House Majority Whip Representative Steve Scalise (R-LA) stated, "You've seen an exposure of what I think is a lot of corruption and real concerns that have been raised about the special counsel. In fact, just the credibility of the special counsel is very much in question. Because, as you mentioned, so many of the people that Mueller brought in, the people working on that, were very anti-Trump in the campaign, and still to this day. ... So, I think just the impartiality of this investigation has been called into question, and I have some real serious concerns about it."[327]

Calling this a witch-hunt is giving witch-hunts a bad rap. Personally I believe all of this is part of a silent coup designed to bring down the President. Planned and executed by the Deep State. To be forewarned is to be forearmed. As this parody of justice continues at least no one

---

[327] Hanchett, I., *Breitbart*, 1-4-18, accessed 6-21-19 https://www.breitbart.com/clips/2018/01/04/gop-whip-scalise-the-credibility-of-the-special-counsel-is-very-much-in-question/

can say we haven't known what was going on and what is coming.

Dispatch Forty-three

Avoid the Amnesty Trap

This is a plea to President Trump to stand by his promises and avoid the amnesty trap that the Progressives are trying to lure him into.

Instead lead the congressional forces of those who want to make America great again. Use every tool, every power you have to enact the fo0llowing:

1. Ending chain migration and the visa lottery

2. Mandating employer use of E-Verify[328]

3. Construction of a southern border wall

4. Interior enforcement of immigration law.

---

[328] E-Verify, accessed 6-21-19 https://www.e-verify.gov/

Drain the Swamp

Rarely do things that don't make sense on a personal level suddenly make sense on a national level.

Look at preemptive war. If hitting someone back first doesn't make sense in the neighborhood how can it shine like a beacon of sanity in the councils of state?

Think about a family dinner party. You invite your family, maybe a few friends, you plan the menu, cook the meal and them when you serve it people you don't know, who weren't invited and many of whom don't even like you crowd in at the table. Does it make sense to just act like this is acceptable? When the uninvited begin taking food away from your own children would you be hateful, a bigot, a racist if you asked them to leave?

Why does it make sense to lock our homes at night, to have security systems, to have a fence around the White House but to leave the borders of our homeland unguarded?

President Trump, your enemies are attempting to get you to back amnesty for the so-called Dreamers. They are doing this in an effort to divorce you from your base. They have got to make the millions who support you turn their backs for their plot to impeach you to succeed.

You seem to be in tune with those of us out here in fly-over country. Read our lips, "NO AMNESTY!"

Any amnesty bill passed will be used by the Progressives to bring in more and more and more. The courts will block any restrictions and stretch the open door. These undocumented democrats will eventually bring in millions of mothers, fathers, brothers, sisters, cousins and third cousins twice removed. Passing a DACA amnesty will be the breaking point of no return.

Save yourself. Save us all from drowning in a sea of the other. America can't be great again if America is going to slip beneath the waves of a migration tsunami.

America already accepts more refugees than the rest of the world combined. We have more legal immigration than any other nation. We have tens f millions of illegal immigrants. We are one of only 30 nations out of more than 190 that allow birthright citizenship. Anchor babies (just think about what that name implies) and birth tourism flies in the face of reason.

Instead of a Progressive sponsored Trojan horse meant to import millions of democrat voters actively work to pass the RAISE Act. I will recommend this course of action by quoting you,

For decades, the United States was operated and has operated a very low-skilled immigration system, issuing record numbers of Green Cards to low-wage immigrants. This policy has placed substantial pressure on American workers, taxpayers and community resources. Among those hit the hardest in recent years have been immigrants and, very importantly, minority workers competing for jobs against brand-new arrivals. And it has not been fair to our people, to our citizens, to our workers.

The RAISE Act ends chain migration, and replaces our low-skilled system with a new points-based system for receiving a Green

Card. This competitive application process will favor applicants who can speak English, financially support themselves and their families, and demonstrate skills that will contribute to our economy.[329]

Personally I believe we need a moratorium on immigration for ten years. That would give us the breathing space to clear out the illegals and assimilate the legal.

Don't let McConnell and Ryan lead you down the primrose path. Neither of them have your best interest at heart.

Obama called us clingers. Hillary called us despicable. The terrorists call us infidels. You called us Americans. We took that and you to heart. We believe your promises especially your promise to end the migration invasion. Stand by that promise. It is fundamental in the quest to make America great again and don't fall into the amnesty trap.

---

[329] Numbers USA, 1—3-17, accessed https://www.numbersusa.com/resource-article/raise-act

BUILD THE WALL! BUILD THE WALL! BUILD THE WALL!

How? Put a 5% surcharge on all wire transfers of money overseas and let the illegals pay for the wall. However you do it Mr. President ... do it. This is what got you elected.

How? You are the Commander-in-Chief. Order the United States Naval Construction Battalions, better known as the Seabees and the Army Corps of Engineers to build the wall. They are some of the best builders in the world. They are trained and equipped to build anything. They are already fully funded. Instead of building schools, hospitals, and gas stations in Afghanistan for the Taliban to burn down have them build the wall.

Don't listen to people who were against you from day one and are still against you now. All they want is cheap labor, democrat votes, and to divorce you from your base.

Listen instead to those who supported you at the ballot box and who support you still.

Protect our homes, families, and jobs by giving us a level playing field. End the migration invasion and make America great again.

BUILD THE WALL! BUILD THE WALL! BUILD THE WALL!

Just one last thing to think about Mr. President; don't let amnesty become your "Read my Lips" moment.

Dispatch Forty-four

DACA Will Never Be Enough

The movement to legalize the illegal will never stop until the untold millions of undocumented democrats have the right to vote. Eternally shopping for the a perpetual majority so they can finish the work of fundamentally transforming America the Progressives agitate ceaselessly for amnesty.

If DACA is ever passed it will become the vehicle for millions of low information voters dependent on the government to overflow our system in a tsunami of votes for bigger government. The courts will stretch it to cover anyone and everyone.

If we don't have merit based immigration system what do we have? If we don't pick the best and the brightest who do we pick? If we don't bring in people who will be a benefit to our society who are we bringing in? Are we instead bringing in those without merit, the worst and the dimmest, and those who are a drag on the system? Oh yes, that sounds like a prescription for success.

Illegal aliens and open borders activists with "United We Dream," a group that is partially funded by globalist billionaire George Soros has been staging demonstrations around the country.[330] Does anyone else find it interesting that people who are in our country illegally can openly demonstrate, march, and protest and nothing ever happens to them?

Here are some examples of how ridiculous this has become:

Illegal alien activists held a mock funeral in the U.S. Senate rotunda, saying that because Congress and President Trump have not given them amnesty, "they are killing our dreams."

---

[330] King, J., *The Fifth Column*, 11-17-16, accessed 6-21-19 https://thefifthcolumnnews.com/2016/11/the-evidence-of-soros-funded-protesters/

John Binder of Breitbart reports, "A group of mostly illegal aliens and open borders activists with the group "United We Dream" gathered in the Senate rotunda on Wednesday to demand an immediate passage of a full-scale, expansive amnesty plan that would potentially give legal status and a pathway to U.S. citizenship to all of the 12 to 30 million illegal aliens living in the U.S."[331]

AND:

Illegal aliens charged into pro-amnesty Sen. Thom Tillis' (R-NC) Senate office on Capitol Hill demanding an immediate amnesty for all 12 to 30 million illegal aliens living in the United States, hurling insults in the process.

As the group of illegal aliens and open borders activists — with the George Soros-funded group "United We Dream" — stormed Tillis' office demanding amnesty, one illegal alien from North Carolina

---

[331] Binder, J., *Breitbart*, 1-24-18, accessed 6-21-19 https://www.breitbart.com/politics/2018/01/24/killing-dreams-illegal-aliens-hold-mock-funeral-u-s-senate/?utm_source=newsletter&utm_medium=email&utm_term=daily&utm_content=links&utm_campaign=20180124

shouted, "F*ck this conservative! F*ck this person!"[332]

Do things like that sound over the top to you or is just me? How can we allow people who are here illegally to invade our government offices and attempt to intimidate our representatives into making their illegal actions legal? What about the rule of law.

What's next? Will thieves storm police stations to hold demonstrations demanding that theft is made legal?

[332] _____., *Breitbart*, 1-24-18, accessed https://www.breitbart.com/politics/2018/01/24/fck-conservative-fck-person-illegal-aliens-charge-pro-amnesty-thom-tillis-senate-office/?utm_source=newsletter&utm_medium=email&utm_term=daily&utm_content=links&utm_campaign=20180124

Drain the Swamp

Dispatch Forty-five

America Off to the Races

Will Mueller and his Clintonista hit squad
manage to entrap President Trump in
perjury before he can prod the DOJ to do a
serious investigation of the Clinton mob? In
other words will the Silent Coup succeed in
overthrowing the President before the
President can get his Deep State infected
DOJ to carry out a serious investigation of
the Obama-Clinton-FBI CABAL that has
been conspiring since before last year's
election to fix the outcome and since to
nullify the results. That is the question.

On the Silent Coup front:

The Mueller persecution continues to pursue
President Trump to testify under oath, a
pre-requisite to springing his perjury trap.
The President's supporters hope and pray
that he isn't led to do so. If his lawyers

suggest it they should be sued for malpractice. Instead he should do as Cli9nton did. Ask for the questions in writing and respond in writing. That way it isn't under oath and everything can be vetted seven ways to sundown before it is transmitted to the inquisition.

On the trail of the plotters:

President Trump has called for the de-classification and release to the public of the FISA Memo.[333] It hasn't happened yet.

Trump has called for a renewed investigation of Hillary's email debacle.[334] It is moving a glacier-like pace. You would have to drive a stake in the ground next to it to see if it is moving at all.

Trump has called for a renewed investigation of that money-laundering

---

[333] Moore, M., *The New York Post*, 1-28-18, accessed 6-22-19 https://nypost.com/2018/01/28/white-house-confirms-trump-wants-to-release-classified-fbi-memo/

[334] Sabur, R., *The Telegraph*, 1-5-18, accessed https://www.telegraph.co.uk/news/2018/01/05/hillary-clinton-faces-fresh-investigations-amid-renewed-corruption/

scheme of New York's sixth crime family, the Clinton Foundation.[335] We haven't heard anything new happening here yet.

Following tweets and statements from President Trump concerning the Uranium One deal between Hillary's State Department and Russia the DOJ is supposedly looking into whether this was a case of classic Clinton pay-for-play.[336]

All of this is of course being slow walked by the Deep State in the DOJ and the FBI. The Obama holdovers and the left leaning civil service have the President in their cross hairs as he attempts to grab them by the short hairs.

In this race between the Mueller Star Chamber and our Star we all know which side the Progressive establishment in Congress, the courts, the media, and the civil service is on. There are only us, the

[335] Goldman, A., *The New York Times*, 1-5-18, accessed https://www.nytimes.com/2018/01/05/us/politics/clinton-foundation-fbi.html
[336] Price, G. *Newsweek*, 12-21-17, accessed 6-22-19 https://www.newsweek.com/uranium-trump-justice-fbi-clinton-755066

Drain the Swamp

Deplorables out here in fly-over country cheering on the first leader we've found who doesn't shrink in the face of the left and their full court press. Let the President know that you support him. Call the White House (202-456-1111), send him an email https://www.whitehouse.gov/contact/, or write him a letter: President Trump, The White House, 1600 Pennsylvania Avenue NW, Washington, DC 20500.

Drain the Swamp

Dispatch Forty-six

The Second Amendment
Means What It Says

In the words of AWR Hawkins in Breitbart
"When the Second Amendment was ratified
in 1791 the phrase, 'well-regulated militia,'
underlined the importance of the words,
'shall not be infringed.'"[337]

The Second Amendment says, "A well-
regulated militia, being necessary to the
security of a free state, the right of the
people to keep and bear arms, shall not be
infringed."

It must be remembered that the shot heard
round the world which ignited the
Revolution was fought by local militias at
Lexington and Concord standing strong

---

[337] Hawkins, A., *Breitbart*, 2-1-18, accessed 6-22-19
https://www.breitbart.com/2nd-
amendment/2018/02/01/a-well-regulated-militia-
private-gun-ownership/

against the regular army troops of the greatest empire in the world. Without those militias and the privately held guns that made them possible there would have been no Revolution. Because without those militias and the privately held guns that made them possible the colonists would have had no means to resist the tyranny of the king.

To rightly understand the meaning of the Second Amendment first we need to understand, "What is the meaning of *a militia*." In the majority opinion for *District of Columbia v Heller* (2008), Justice Antonin Scalia explained:[338]

Unlike armies and navies, which Congress is given the power to create ("to raise . . . Armies"; "to provide . . . a Navy," Art. I, §8, cls. 12–13), the militia is assumed by Article I already to be in existence. Congress is given the power to "provide for calling forth the militia," S8, cl. 15; and the power not to create, but to "organiz[e]" it—and not to organize "a" militia, which is what one would expect if the militia were to be a

---

[338] Ibid.

federal creation, but to organize "the" militia, connoting a body already in existence, ibid., cl. 16. This is fully consistent with the ordinary definition of the militia as all able-bodied men. From that pool, Congress has plenary power to organize the units that will make up an effective fighting force.

We also need to examine what the Founders and Framers meant when they spoke of a militia. When to attempting to explain that the American citizenry had within itself the authority to band together for purposes of repelling tyranny James Madison in Federalist 46[339] he clearly stated that "ultimate authority... resides in the people alone."[340]

That he meant this as a guarantee to the people of the means with which to resist tyranny on the part of the government is

---

[339] Hakins, AWR, *Breitbart*, 7-6-14, accessed 6-22-19
https://www.breitbart.com/politics/2014/07/06/fede
ralist-46-americans-exceptional-because-armed/
[340] Federalist No. 46, accessed 6-22-19
https://www.congress.gov/resources/display/content
/The+Federalist+Papers#TheFederalistPapers-46

clear when he goes on to say, "Extravagant as the supposition is, let it however be made. Let a regular army, fully equal to the resources of the country, be formed; and let it be entirely at the devotion of the federal government; still it would not be going too far to say, that the State governments, with the people on their side, would be able to repel the danger."[341]

Here's what President Trump has to say on the subject:[342]

The Second Amendment to our Constitution is clear. The right of the people to keep and bear Arms shall not be infringed upon. Period.

The Second Amendment guarantees a fundamental right that belongs to all law-abiding Americans. The Constitution doesn't create that right it ensures that the government can't take it away. Our Founding Fathers knew, and our Supreme

---

[341] Ibid.
[342] Hawkins, AWR, *Breitbart*, 8-26-16, accessed 6-22-19
https://www.breitbart.com/politics/2016/08/26/donald-trump-right-to-keep-and-bear-arms-protects-all-our-other-rights/

Court has upheld, that the Second Amendment's purpose is to guarantee our right to defend ourselves and our families. This is about self-defense, plain and simple.

It's been said that the Second Amendment is America's first freedom. That's because the Right to Keep and Bear Arms protects all our other rights. We are the only country in the world that has a Second Amendment. Protecting that freedom is imperative.

Gun and magazine bans are a total failure. That's been proven every time it's been tried. Opponents of gun rights try to come up with scary sounding phrases like "assault weapons", "military-style weapons" and "high capacity magazines" to confuse people. What they're really talking about are popular semi-automatic rifles and standard magazines that are owned by tens of millions of Americans. Law-abiding people should be allowed to own the firearm of their choice. The government has no business dictating what types of firearms good, honest people are allowed to own.

The right of self-defense doesn't stop at the end of your driveway. That's why I have a concealed carry permit and why tens of millions of Americans do too. That permit should be valid in all 50 states. A driver's license works in every state, so it's common sense that a concealed carry permit should work in every state. If we can do that for driving which is a privilege, not a right then surely we can do that for concealed carry, which is a right, not a privilege.

I don't know about you but I have been waiting to hear an American leader say these things for my whole life.

Sic semper tyrannis![343]

---

[343] "Thus Always to Tyrants"

Dispatch Forty-seven

This Obumer Hangover Just Won't Go Away

One of the primary accusations against President Nixon that caused him to resign was that even though he was never shown to be personally aware of any abuses committed in his name he fostered an environment that encouraged such behavior.

The truth is finally seeing the light of day.[344] And what do we see? That President Obama was if not personally complicit in the growing list of abuses exposed he set the tone and offered cover for his minions as they ran amuck trashing the FBI, the CIA, the IRS, FISA, and any other agency that could advance his transformative agenda, secure the nomination for Hillary, and

---

[344] Crowly, M., *The Hill*, 2-12-18, accessed 6-22-19 https://thehill.com/opinion/white-house/373379-federal-abuses-a-growing-blight-on-obamas-legacy

thwart Trump's nomination, election, and administration.

The weaponization of these powerful government agencies shows an administration determined to steal first a primary then an election. So far emails and messages implicate James Comey, Loretta Lynch, Andrew McCabe, Andrew Weissmann, Sally Yates, Peter Strzok, Lisa Page, Bruce Ohr.

Tom Del Beccaro, an attorney and contributor to *Forbes* said, "Holistic analysis of the Justice Department (DOJ) and FBI's interconnected and ostensible investigations of Hillary Clinton and Donald Trump amount to the worst abuse of political power in American history related to elections."[345] And "The DOJ [and] the entire Obama administration wound down the Hillary email crisis in time for her to really run for office and then ramped up the attacks on

---

[345] Kraychik, R., *Breitbart*, 2-9-18, accessed 6-22-19 https://www.breitbart.com/radio/2018/02/09/tom-del-beccaro-corrupt-doj-fbi-roads-lead-obama/

candidate Trump to stop him from being president."[346]

As quoted in an article by Robert Kraychik posted in *Breitbart* Del Beccaro continues, "The FBI was sort of just going through the motions with Hillary, and it's about March or April, and suddenly the election heats up, and Obama goes on TV,[347] and he says, with Chris Wallace, basically, that she didn't intend to do anything [wrong]; she didn't want to harm us,"[348] said Del Beccaro. "That's irrelevant to the crime she committed of possessing classified information in an insecure environment. So he announces this, and once he does, the DOJ and the FBI then change their speed [of] work and the manner in which they're working, the things that they're doing, and between April and June, they exonerate her, and what I mean by that is they change the

---

[346] Ibid.
[347] Fox News 4-10-16, accessed 6-22-19 https://www.foxnews.com/transcript/exclusive-president-barack-obama-on-fox-news-sunday
[348] Kraychik, R., *Breitbart*, 2-9-18, accessed 6-22-19 https://www.breitbart.com/radio/2018/02/09/tom-del-beccaro-corrupt-doj-fbi-roads-lead-obama/

language[349] in the memo as to whether she was doing something wrong from 'gross negligence' of a crime to ... 'extreme carelessness.' That's irrelevant. That's not legal language: 'extreme carelessness.'"[350]

As his evaluation of the situation continued Del Beccaro stated, "Early May, [Obama] endorses her, [and] it's very rare in our history for a president to endorse in a divided primary within his own party,"[351] said Del Beccaro. "If there wasn't a sham investigation going on, why would he take a risk endorsing a candidate under investigation by the FBI when on its face she broke the law? His first appearance with her [was] on the afternoon of July 5.[352] You know what happened on the morning of July

---

[349] Moran, S., *Breitbart*, 1-4-18, accessed 6-22-19 https://www.breitbart.com/politics/2018/01/04/com eys-original-hillary-clinton-email-memo-suggested-possible-felony-violations/

[350] McCarthy, A., *National Review*, 7-5-16, accessed 6-22-19 https://www.nationalreview.com/corner/fbi-rewrites-federal-law-let-hillary-hook/

[351] Kraychik, R., *Breitbart*, 2-9-18, accessed 6-22-19 https://www.breitbart.com/radio/2018/02/09/tom-del-beccaro-corrupt-doj-fbi-roads-lead-obama/

[352] C-Span, 7-5-16, accessed 6-22-19 https://www.c-span.org/video/?412145-1/president-obama-campaigns-hillary-clinton&vod

5? James Comey goes on TV to exonerate her.[353] This cannot be coincidental."[354]

"Seems pretty much like they knew what they were doing to me, don't you think?" asked Del Beccaro, rhetorically.

In what may soon be a growing chorus Rep. Matt Gaetz (R-FL) has called for a second special counsel to investigate abuse at the Department of Justice and the FBI.[355] This seems like a no-brainer since in any honest or realistic scenario it is obvious that the FBI and the DOJ cannot investigate themselves.

When on Fox News Channel's "Watters' World" Gaetz was asked if given Sessions' recusal he had the authority to appoint such a special counsel. Rep. Gaetz answered,

---

[353] _____, accessed 6-22-19 https://www.c-span.org/video/?412231-1/fbi-director-james-comey-criminal-prosecution-not-appropriate-hillary-clinton-email-case

[354] Kraychik, R., *Breitbart*, 2-9-18, accessed 6-22-19 https://www.breitbart.com/radio/2018/02/09/tom-del-beccaro-corrupt-doj-fbi-roads-lead-obama/

[355] Poor, J., *Breitbart*, 2-10-18, accessed 6-22-19 https://www.breitbart.com/clips/2018/02/10/gop-rep-gaetz-calls-appointment-second-special-counsel-fbi-doj-cannot-investigate/

"Of course, he does," Gaetz replied. "There was no legal obligation for that recusal, and frankly, I don't even know what the four corners of that recusal are. Here, the accusation is not against Russia. It is against the very agency that Jeff Sessions leads, the Department of Justice, and then some of the senior politicized leadership at the FBI. So he could appoint that special counsel. More than two dozen Republicans have joined me in calling for it, and it is darn time that it happened."

Now is the time to demand accountability. Let the chips fall where they may. It certainly appears as if these wannabe banana boat authoritarians were attempting to corrupt our election process. They succeeded against Bernie. However, once they failed in the general election they are now attempting to orchestrate a coup against the sitting President.

We cannot allow this to happen. We must let our representatives and senators know we want a Special Counsel to investigate these abuses. You can use this link (https://www.usa.gov/elected-officials) to find out how to contact your representatives and senators. Let them know *We the People* want our country back, we want to drain the swamp, and we want anyone no matter how high prosecuted to the fullest extent of the law for trying to undermine our Republic.

Dispatch Forty-eight

DNC Hack Wasn't A Hack

President Trump tweeted, "I never said Russia did not meddle in the election, I said 'It may be Russia, or China or another country or group, or it may be a 400 pound genius sitting in bed and playing with his computer.' The Russian 'hoax' was that the Trump campaign colluded with Russia. It never did!"[356]

Kim Dotcom has said, "Let me assure you, the DNC hack wasn't even a hack. It was an insider with a memory stick. I know this because I know who did it and why. Special Counsel Mueller is not interested in my evidence. My lawyers wrote to him twice. He never replied."

---

[356] Twitter, accessed 6-22-19 https://twitter.com/realdonaldtrump/status/9652025 56204003328

Dotcom's assertion is backed up by an analysis done last year by a researcher who goes by the name *Forensicator*, who determined that the DNC files were copied at 22.6 MB/s - a speed virtually impossible to achieve from halfway around the world, much less over a local network - yet a speed typical of file transfers to a memory stick.[357]

The local transfer theory of course blows the Russian hacking narrative out of the water, lending credibility to the theory that the DNC "hack" was in fact an inside job, potentially implicating late DNC IT staffer, Seth Rich.

John Podesta's email was allegedly successfully "hacked" (he fell victim to a phishing scam)[358] in March 2016, while the DNC reported suspicious activity (the

---

[357] Vos, E., *Disobedient Media*, 7-9-17, accessed 6-22-19 https://disobedientmedia.com/2017/07/new-research-shows-guccifer-2-0-files-were-copied-locally-not-hacked/
[358] Uchill, J., *The Hill*, 12-13-16, accessed 6-22-19 https://thehill.com/policy/cybersecurity/310234-typo-may-have-caused-podesta-email-hack

suspected Seth Rich file transfer) in late April, 2016.[359]

On May 18, 2017, Dotcom proposed that if Congress includes the Seth Rich investigation in their Russia probe, he would provide written testimony with evidence that Seth Rich was WikiLeaks' source.[360]

And it isn't just Kim Dotcom who has come to this realization. Patrick Lawrence has stated back in 2017 in the magazine *Nation*, "There was no hack of the Democratic National Committee's system on July 5 last year—not by the Russians, not by anyone else. Hard science now demonstrates it was a leak—a download executed locally with a memory key or a similarly portable data-storage device. In short, it was an inside job by someone with access to the DNC's system. This casts serious doubt on the initial "hack," as alleged, that led to the very consequential publication of a large

---

[359] Durden, T., *Zerohedge*, 2-20-18, accessed 6-22-19 https://www.zerohedge.com/news/2018-02-18/kim-dotcom-let-me-assure-you-dnc-hack-wasnt-even-hack
[360] Ibid.

store of documents on WikiLeaks last summer."[361]

Remember the DNC never allowed the FBI to examine their computers.[362] Instead they hired a private company Crowdstrike.[363] Another thing to remember is that what the hack revealed was that Hillary had taken over the DNC and fixed the primary against poor Bernie. This was later corroborated by former Clinton supporter and DNC Chair. But instead of dealing with the substance of the emails as usual the Clinton Crime Family threw up a smoke screen that their media lapdogs helped propagate. Even Bernie helped out taking any discussion of the emails off the table during a debate at the height of the primary season.

---

[361] Lawrence, P., *The Nation*, 8-9-17, accessed 6-22-19 https://www.thenation.com/article/a-new-report-raises-big-questions-about-last-years-dnc-hack/
[362] Ibid.
[363] Caruso, J., *The Daily Caller*, 6-24-17, accessed 6-22-19 https://dailycaller.com/2017/06/24/crowdstrike-five-things-everyone-is-ignoring-about-the-russia-dnc-story/

Hillary didn't dispute the charges instead following the rules laid down by her philosophical guide, Saul Alinsky she misdirected and covered it up with the BIG lie, "The Russians did it."[364]

This alleged DNC hack served as the very beginning of the Russiagate coup that is slow walking the impeachment of President Trump.[365]

It's past time for every American citizen who truly wants to Make America Great Again to stand up and be counted. Contact your senators. Contact your representatives and let them know you want then to pull the plug on this baseless investigation.

There are plenty of other things we could investigate. For instance:

---

[364] Adams, D.L., *New English Review*, 1-10, accessed 6-22-19
https://www.newenglishreview.org/DL_Adams/Saul_Alinsky_and_the_Rise_of_Amorality_in_American_Politics/
[365] Maté, A. *The Nation*, 10-8-17, accessed 6-22-19
https://www.thenation.com/article/russiagate-is-more-fiction-than-fact/

Drain the Swamp

Benghazi

Fast and Furious

The Missing emails

Uranium One

The corruption at the IRS and the FBI under the Obama regime

Loretta Lynch and the tarmac sit-down with the Don of New York's sixth crime family

Instead of trying to hang the new sheriff in town let's drain the swamp.

Drain the Swamp

Dispatch Forty-nine

Quit Disarming Teachers

As one of the millions of teachers in America I know there is one thing I don't ever want to be...a fish in a barrel.

Think of the hero teachers who've thrown their bodies in front of students taking bullets fired by mentally deranged mass murders. If these heroes had had a weapon does anyone doubt they would've used it to protect those students? Aspiring mass murders who seek out gun free zones to commit their atrocities are inherent cowards. And they're also untrained and unprepared for anyone with the ability to stand up to them. As soon as someone with a gun shows up they either kill themselves or die.

Gun free zones are a neon target painted on our children. If you notice there has never been a mass shooting at a police station. These maniacs avoid any place where someone might shoot back.

It isn't guns that are killing people deranged criminals are. A criminal's preferred target is an unarmed victim. No one is talking about turning the teaching staff of any school into a militia. No one is talking about forcing any teacher to carry a gun. What people are talking about is not disarming teachers who are already or who could be legally licensed to carry a weapon and who have the desire to do so.

Some schools in Arkansas not only allow people with concealed carry permits to carry on school grounds they provide training and weapons to those who would like to do so and they also organize these teachers, administrators, and support personnel into a security force prepared to react if the need arises. They also publicize this and post signs letting the would-be killers know that they won't find a soft target and instead of shooting sheep they may encounter a shepherd with the ability to put them in the cross-hairs.[366]

And Arkansas isn't alone. In Texas 172 school districts presently arm selected teachers.[367] Today eighteen states allow adults to carry guns with some form of school approval.[368] Kentucky[369] is considering a law that would establish a marshal program to help teachers get a license to carry on campus.[370]

Instead of a target on our schools perhaps a sign such as the one posted outside an Arkansas school which says, "Please be aware that certain staff members are armed and may use whatever force is necessary to protect our students" would go a long way towards reducing school shootings.

---

[366] Chavez, N., CNN, 2-28-18, accessed 6-22-19 https://www.cnn.com/2018/02/24/us/armed-teachers-states-trnd/index.html
[367] Inverse, accessed 6-22-19 https://www.inverse.com/article/41606-which-states-allow-teachers-to-carry-guns
[368] Ibid.
[369] Ibid.
[370] Barton, R., NPR, 2-19-18, accessed 6-22-19 https://www.npr.org/2018/02/19/587121635/propos al-to-allow-guns-in-kentucky-schools

Dispatch Fifty

Today is Yesterday's Tomorrow

Science fiction has predicted many of today's realities from cell phones to tablets. Many things that are today part of History like walking on the moon, organ transplants, and space stations were once flights of fancy.

Futurists build current events on a foundation of History to provide a launching pad for visions of what is to come. One of the most widely recognized Futurists is Alvin Toffler whose seminal works include Future Shock and The Third Wave. He is also the one who told us, "Change is not merely necessary to life - it is life."[371]

Have you ever heard of Ray Kurzweil?

---

[371] Brainyquote, accessed 6-22-19
https://www.brainyquote.com/authors/alvin_toffler

If you haven't you are about to.

The Wall Street Journal has described Kurzweil as "the restless genius." Forbes calls him "the ultimate thinking machine." He has been ranked by Inc. Magazine as #8 among entrepreneurs in the United States He has also been called "the rightful heir to Thomas Edison," while according to PBS he is one of 16 "revolutionaries who made America."

His inventions are breathtaking and they impact our lives on a daily basis. These inventions include the first CCD flat-bed scanner, the first omni-font optical character recognition, the first print-to-speech reading machine for the blind, the first text-to-speech synthesizer, the first music synthesizer capable of recreating the grand piano and other orchestral instruments, and the first commercially marketed large-vocabulary speech recognition.[372]

---

[372] Kurzweil Technologies, accessed 6-22-19 http://www.kurzweiltech.com/aboutray.html

Drain the Swamp

Here is my question for today "Is Ray Kurzweil a futurist?"

Today, many websites attribute Mr. Kurzweil with accurate predictions about where the world will be tomorrow. In his latest book, *The Singularity is Near* he describes the singularity as, a reference to the theoretical limitlessness of exponential expansion) that will see the merging of our biology with the staggering achievements of "GNR" (genetics, nanotechnology, and robotics) to create a species of unrecognizably high intelligence, durability, comprehension, memory and so on. This is a bold prediction; however, bold predictions do not a Futurist make.

There is a fundamental difference between someone who is a professional writer and observer of humanity such as Toffler and someone who is a technological genius with almost unlimited resources who is actively working to make his predictions reality. Toffler reads studies and interviews on his way to predictions of where society and technologies will go next. Kurzweil traded in his massive private business built upon his inventions to become Google's Director of Engineering whose sole job is to make the company's computers smarter than humans.[373] He is working every day to improve artificial intelligence and then wed that to cutting edge robotics and human interface to produce the very singularity he is predicting.[374]

Reaching back to the science fiction genre which I referenced earlier we are looking at the rise of the machines, the coming of the cylons, skynet, and the matrix. These of course are all fiction; however, the reality we face brings this question to my mind, "Once we design and build machines that are smarter than we are and they design and build machines that are smarter than they are what do they need us for?"

The projected development of Artificial Intelligence (AI) foresees a time when machines not only rival but surpass human capabilities. Once this happens will we

---

[373] McGee, M., SEO, 2-25-14, accessed 6-22-19 https://searchengineland.com/ray-kurzweils-job-google-beat-ibms-watson-natural-language-search-185149
[374] Ibid.

know when these super intelligent machines cross the threshold from hyper abilities to self-awareness? These scenarios are troubling, even terrifying yet most people would dismiss them as the science fiction they mirror. There is another aspect of this technological revolution that is not quite as far-fetched and not quite as unbelievable: automation.

We have lived with automation all of our lives. People have been displaced by innovation since the Sumerian water wheel took the place of people with buckets bringing water from rivers into their fields. I can remember people telling me in the 1970s, "I'm a keypunch operator, I'll always have a job." Today machinists, tool and dye makers, auto workers, and many people have been replaced by machines. Tomorrow white collar workers will face the same fate as so many of their blue collar brethren.[375] Why do we need accountants when machines can fill in the same programs they use today to figure taxes

---

[375] Walters, R., *Financial Times*, 3-3-14, accessed 6-22-19 https://www.ft.com/content/dc895d54-a2bf-11e3-9685-00144feab7de#axzz2vnXoaFPR

and current accounts? Who needs teachers
when lectures can be delivered by speech
technology, questions answered by Watson
type question answers, and tests grade
themselves?

Look to Futurists like Toffler who are
predicting where we are headed and look to
inventors like Kurzweil who are telegraphing
where they are headed and a collage of
futures points to the tomorrow today will
become.

It is my contention that we as a people, as
a society, and as a civilization need to
address this soon approaching brave new
world. When I speak to people about these
coming changes the almost universal
reaction is, "Not in my lifetime." I believe
this is a combination of wishful thinking,
hiding our heads in the sand, and having no
idea what is going on around us.

This is a social dislocation approaching at
speeds unforeseen. I don't believe these
changes are decades away. I believe within
a decade they will be upon us. Large
percentages of blue and white collar
workers will be displaced. Machines will

take the place of humans in many areas and humans will not be able to compete with them. If we allow this to come upon us with no preparation we will be swamped by the rising tide of change and drowned in the tsunami of innovation.

Change is accelerating as the interconnectedness of communication accelerates the cross-polarization of ideas. After tens of thousands of years the use of the wheel had not spread all the way around the world. Today something is invented in America this morning, improved in India this afternoon, and spawning new ideas tomorrow in China. We cannot contain the explosion of technology because someone somewhere will always seek to move beyond the known to the unknown. No matter what glories we have beheld yesterday tomorrow is coming whether today is ready or not.

Long ago Toffler told us, "Future shock is the shattering stress and disorientation that we induce in individuals by subjecting them to too much change in too short a time."[376] He also predicted and predated Kurzweil's Singularity when he said, "The next major explosion is going to be when genetics and computers come together. I'm talking about an organic computer - about biological substances that can function like a semiconductor."[377]

How long will it before our cars drive themselves, 3-D printers create human organs, and the government has the ability to monitor everyone at once? How long will it be before you cannot tell the difference between speaking to a computer on the phone and speaking to a human?

Failure to plan is planning to fail. If we as a society do not stop living in yesterday and face up to the challenges of today we will sacrifice our future.

And always remember, it's tough to make predictions, especially about the future.

---

[376] Brainyquote, accessed 6-22-19
https://www.brainyquote.com/authors/alvin_toffler
[377] Brainyquote, accessed 6-22-19
https://www.brainyquote.com/authors/alvin_toffler

Drain the Swamp

Dispatch Fifty-one

Once Again Sing the Chorus
Build the Wall Build the Wall Build the Wall

In the last presidential election we had the choice between the last nail in our coffin and a chance. We now have a chance. America's place on the world stage is being clarified by President Trump. But we need to keep things in perspective.

We need to keep our eye on the prize. What good does it do to gain the world if we lose the homeland? It was mainly domestic issues that drove everyone to the polls to prevent Hillary's coronation. We want America back. We want the shining city on a hill back not the shabby globalist collective Obama, Hillary and the rest of the Progressives have been shoving down our throat.

We need to save our country from disappearing beneath the waves of the uninvited. And to have any chance of doing that we need to have a country left to save not just a place with open borders and a sign that says, "No admission fee and everything's free."

The clock is ticking. The courts have shown they will do everything they can to stop our president from enforcing sanity or even the law to stop the invasion. Congress has shown they will spend money on anything except border security.

Stop the migration invasion! Secure the border! No amnesty!

Bring our troops home from around the world and let them make us secure. Build the wall, build the wall, build the wall.

Those who say we cannot build a wall need to take a look at the border between North and South Korea.[378] It may not be a

---

[378] Google, Korea DMZ, accessed 6-22-19 https://www.google.com/search?q=korea+dmz&tbm =isch&tbo=u&source=univ&sa=X&ved=0ahUKEwiW1 eCy9bPWAhUP2mMKHTXkBAAQiR4ItAE&biw=1333&b ih=618

smaller version of the Great Wall but it's effective. Or look at the wall Israel built on their border with the Palestinian Authority.[379] If these secure borders can be built, guarded, and maintained why can't we do the same thing on our Southern border?

Bring our troops home from Korea. Why should they be there as a trip wire? Their deaths are meant to do nothing else but guarantee that we'll be involved in the next war. Let South Korea, Japan, and Taiwan deal with the suicidal Rocket Man. Their populations and economies are much larger than the gulag which is North Korea.

Bring our troops home from Germany. Lately the Germans and French seem friendlier to Russia than they do to us so who are we protecting them from? Themselves?

Why should we spend billions each year to maintain these garrison troops left over

---

[379] Google, Israeli Wall, accessed 6-22-19 https://www.google.com/search?q=israeli+wall&tbm=isch&tbo=u&source=univ&sa=X&ved=0ahUKEwit4pTb9bPWAhVD8WMKHYz7AO8QiR4IrwE&biw=1333&bih=618

from wars fought more than a half century ago. Instead of spending that money overseas post the troops to our southern border and spend that money in our own country.

DACA is a Trojan horse. Give amnesty to anyone and you'll end up giving it to everyone. The minute it becomes law the ACLU, CAIR, LA Raza and all the other America Last front groups will file challenges to the law's supposedly iron-clad limitations. These inevitable law suits will give liberal activist judges the opportunity to prop the door open. They'll argue, "Why is it fair that some get citizenship and others don't?" If the Trump Administration dares to stand against these attempts to stretch a limited amnesty into a come-one-come-all free-for-all the Ninth Circuit will get the opportunity to slap them down and knock the door off its hinges.

Besides, anyone apprehended by ICE after DACA will say they were brought here as a child and the courts will dutifully certify them as unaccompanied minors no matter how old they are.

Drain the Swamp

President Trump, for standing up to the globalists you are to be commended. Out here in fly-over country most are proud to hear you speak for us bravely and forthrightly. Signing the latest Democrat omnibus obscenity has caused major ripples out here in fly-over country. DACA would have pulled the plug.

Here's an election strategy that will appeal to the Deplorables. When the next Porkulous spending bill comes up right before the midterm election veto it, call the electioneering plutocrats back into session and run against a Congress that is thwarting the agenda you were elected to implement, demand full funding for the wall. Better yet demand a 10% tax on money transfers to foreign countries and use that money to build the wall, or use the seized assets of the Mexican drug lords to build the wall. Whatever you do build the wall build the wall, build the wall.

If you complete your reform of the Obamacare health insurance debacle, continue your reformation of the byzantine tax codes, and maintain your excellent record of cutting regulations you'll go down as one of the greatest presidents in our history. However, when a patient is hemorrhaging the first thing to do is stop the bleeding. So first of all as our Commander-in-Chief, the one charged with protecting the nation, build the wall build the wall, build the wall. Few people know the name of Marcus Aurelius. Most people know the name of Hadrian build the wall build the wall, build the wall.

Drain the Swamp

Dispatch Fifty-two

Trump v Mueller Who Gets Who First?

The recent raid by the Robert Mueller's
witch hunters on President Trump's lawyer's
offices shows that we are nearing the third
act.[380] The ever expanding search for a
crime is reportedly now looking into a
campaign donation that was made by a pro-
Russian Ukrainian oligarch to the Trump
Foundation in September 2015.[381] The
donation was reportedly made after then-
candidate Donald Trump gave a 20-minute
speech at a European conference that
promoted closer ties between Ukraine and
the West.

---

[380] Tucker, E. & Chad Day, AP, 4-10-18, accessed 6-
23-19
https://apnews.com/a256631aa1a242e2a7b705e2b6
a5b989
[381] Sheth, S., Business Insider, 4-9-18, accessed
https://www.businessinsider.com/mueller-victor-
pinchuk-trump-foundation-donation-michael-cohen-
2018-4

Let's see Hillary and the Clinton Crime Family get a pass for running a pay-to-play scam out of Foggy Bottom but the Persecutor-in-Chief has to take a microscope to this one donation. Sounds like the creature from the Black Lagoon is alive and well in the Washington swamp.

Leading constitutional lawyer and longtime Harvard professor Alan Dershowitz, in what he considers "a very serious escalation" of the special investigation into Russian interference of the 2016 election, called the FBI's raid of the offices of President Donald Trump's longtime personal attorney Michael Cohen on Monday "a shocking and disturbing development."[382] He added the development "should shock everybody, no matter what part of the partisan divide you're on."

According to Dershowitz, "This is a very dangerous day today for lawyer-client relations." "If this were Hillary Clinton being investigated and they went into her

[382] Patten, D., *Newsmax*, 4-9-18, accessed 6-23-19 https://www.newsmax.com/premium/alan-dershowitz-fbi-raid-michael-cohen/2018/04/09/id/853507/

lawyer's office, the ACLU would be on every television station in America, jumping up and down,"[383] he added. "The deafening silence from the ACLU and civil libertarians about the intrusion into the lawyer-client confidentiality is really appalling,"[384] Dershowitz said. Dershowitz recommended that Trump make a motion in court to take Cohen's materials away from the FBI and make a judge decide what evidence can be used and which cannot.

What do some of the President's allies have to say?

"Time to fire the FBI Director,"[385] a sometime Trump adviser, Roger Stone, said in a tweet.

---

[383] Kasperowicz, P., *The Washington Examiner*, 4-9-18, accessed 6-23-19
https://www.washingtonexaminer.com/news/alan-dershowitz-today-is-a-very-dangerous-day-for-lawyer-client-relations
[384] Ibid.
[385] *Newsmax*, 4-10-18, accessed 6-23-19
https://www.newsmax.com/politics/trump-twitter-cohen-raid/2018/04/10/id/853572/

Other allies suggested that the Mueller investigation has become undisciplined or even criminal.

"It's clear Mr. Mueller's operation has nothing do with fair enforcement of the law or equal justice," Joseph diGenova, a Washington lawyer who agreed to join the president's legal team last month before potential conflicts of interest prevented his hiring, said in an appearance on Fox Business Network. "It is basically a bunch of mobsters."[386]

Congress, he said, should impeach Rosenstein for not complying with an August 2017 subpoena seeking records related to the origin of the investigation into possible collusion between Trump's campaign and Russia.

New York Post writer Michael Goodwin has some things to say about the Mueller witch hunt. "The violent swings of the leaky pendulum make this an excellent moment to call timeout on the Mueller probe. What does he have, where is he going and when

---

[386] Ibid.

is he going to get there?"[387] "Those are basic questions that need to be answered. The American people deserve facts instead of waters muddied by partisanship, innuendo and special access to biased big-media companies."[388] "Given the stakes, the public has a right to know at this point what it all adds up to. If Mueller won't speak for himself, his handler, Rod Rosenstein, the deputy attorney general who created Mueller, should speak for him."[389] "The endless leaks are the final straw. The Mueller probe is the most important investigation in a generation and is casting a cloud over a presidency. If this were a probe involving a third-level bureaucrat, assassination-by-leak would be distasteful but not as meaningful. But this is the presidency, and even Trump haters should be appalled at the shoddy process."[390]

---

[387] Swanson, M., *Newsmax*, 4-9-18, accessed https://www.newsmax.com/newsfront/michael-goodwin-mueller-russia-probe/2018/04/09/id/853434/
[388] Ibid.
[389] Ibid.
[390] Ibid.

Lou Dobbs said, "We're witnessing an orchestrated assault on the President of the United States."[391]

And conservative watchdog Judicial Watch official Tom Fitton on Monday night blasted the Department of Justice as "out of control,"[392] and suggested special counsel Robert Mueller's investigation "ought to be shut down."[393]

What do the Democrats have to say?

"If the president is thinking of using this raid to fire Special Counsel Mueller or otherwise interfere with the chain of command in the Russia probe, we Democrats have one simple message for him: don't,"[394] the Senate Minority Leader Chuck Schumer of New York said in a statement.

---

[391] *Newsmax*, 4-9-18, accessed 6-23-19 https://www.newsmax.com/politics/tom-fitton-judicial-watch-fbi-special-counsel/2018/04/09/id/853530/
[392] Ibid.
[393] Ibid.
[394] *Newsmax*, 4-10-18, accessed 6-23-19 https://www.newsmax.com/politics/trump-twitter-cohen-raid/2018/04/10/id/853572/

And what does President Trump have to say about all this?

"These people have the biggest conflicts of interest I have ever seen. Democrats -- all. Either Democrats or a couple of Republicans who worked for President Obama,"[395] Trump said of the FBI investigators. "They're not looking at the other side -- Hillary Clinton... all of the crimes that were committed, all of the things that happened that everybody is very angry about from the Republican side and the independent side."[396]

"When I saw this, when I heard about it, that is a whole new level of unfairness."[397]

"They found no collusion what so ever with Russia."[398]

"I've wanted to keep it down. I've given over a million pages in documents to the

---

[395] Westwood, S. *The Washington Examiner*, 4-9-18, accessed 6-23-19
https://www.washingtonexaminer.com/news/white-house/trump-decries-witch-hunt-after-fbi-raids-his-attorneys-office
[396] Ibid.
[397] Ibid.
[398] Ibid.

special counsel. They continue to just go forward and here we are talking about Syria, we're talking about a lot of serious things... and I have this witch hunt constantly going on for over 12 months now,"[399] Trump said. "Actually it's much more than that. You could say right after I won the nomination it started."[400]

Or as he tweeted this morning, "Attorney-client privilege is dead!"[401]

And what about those of us out here in fly-over country who voted for and still support our president?

I think what we need now is a private meeting between the President and the Rosenstein-Mueller Cabal where Mr. Trump uses one of his best catch phrases, "You're fired!"

Let the chips fall where they may.

There is a silent coup in progress waged by the government party against a duly elected president. If the creature from the Black

---

[399] Ibid.
[400] Ibid.
[401] Ibid.

Drain the Swamp

Lagoon can manage to lead the denizens of the swamp in overthrowing the man we elected to drain the swamp. The lie will have been exposed America has become a functioning oligarchy disguised as a nonfunctioning democratic republic.

Drain the Swamp

Dispatch Fifty-three

Why I am No Longer
a Conservative Republican

Maybe it's just me but I'm tired of the same
old same old in our politics. The big-box
monopoly parties have morphed into two
sides of the same coin, two heads on the
same bird of prey. Today our choice boils
down to the Conservative Republican tax
and spend, infringe personal liberty, and
outsource or sovereignty policies or the
Liberal Democrat tax and spend, infringe
personal liberty, and outsource or
sovereignty policies. But of course, since we
don't want to throw away our vote we must
vote for one of the big boys. Conservative?
Liberal? Tweedle Dee Or Tweedle Dum?

As a voter I've had my Damascus Road
experience, the scales have fallen from my
eyes, and I have reached the point where I
would rather throw away my vote voting for

someone who might actually try to find a different way to operate our government besides taxing like the Sun King and spending like a drunken sailor. (By the way, do you know the difference between how a drunken sailor spends and how the Republicrats spend? The drunken sailor is spending his own money.)

And what might this different way be? How about this for radical: let's return to constitutional government? WOW! what a concept.

How did we arrive at the current situation? James Madison in his speech to the Virginia Ratifying Convention, June 16, 1788 said, "There are more instances of the abridgement of the freedom of the people by the gradual and silent encroachment of those in power, than by violent and sudden usurpation." We didn't get here all in one jump. First the camel said, "Can I just stick my nose in your tent to stay warm?" and finally the generous man found himself out in the cold as the camel settled down for a nice warm nap, one inch at a time.

Drain the Swamp

The compassion of our people built a safety net for those who needed help, and the greed of the lazy have turned it into a hammock. America, the Land of the Free has turned into America, from each according to their abilities to each according to their need. The willingness to share our heritage has led America to welcome more immigrants each year than the rest of the world combined, and the abuse of our generosity has turned into a migration invasion that threatens to overwhelm us and destroy the future of our children. Taxes imposed to meet the ever-swelling demands of government have turned into a blatant wealth re-distribution program that makes most pyramid schemes look fair. Sometimes I think our government looks at a productive citizen as merely a source of residual income. Or as the ads promise, our leaders lay on the beach of self-importance and our checks just keep pouring in. We are no longer respected as Citizens. Instead, we are coveted as consumers, or human capital.

There is a famous quote often attributed to Albert Einstein, "Insanity: doing the same thing over and over again and expecting different results."[402]

If we want a different world we have to start at the only place we have the absolute sovereign ability to make a change, we must start with ourselves.

I quit the Republican Party once it was obvious that the Republican majority in Congress I had spent my entire adult life working for was just a change in leadership and not a change in direction. I quit calling myself a conservative after the second Bush debacle made it obvious that the conservative movement had been hijacked by the neocons and I realized that you can't defend a captured position. You can't conserve what has already been lost. I realized that we as a people, we as a federation of States need to find a different way.

One thing I know, no one person can do this alone. No one group can do it. To make any headway in the face of the electoral

---

[402] Brainyquote, accessed 6-23-19
https://www.brainyquote.com/quotes/unknown_133
991

monopoly held by the party of power the many third party groups are going to have to coalesce into an effective opposition. We can't let divisions divide us any more, egos will have to be suppressed, and we will have to bond together with everyone dedicated to limited government, personal liberty, and economic freedom.

None of us can roll this big rock up this steep hill by ourselves. However, together we can.

Winston Churchill said, "If you will not fight for the right when you can easily win without bloodshed, if you will not fight when your victory will be sure and not so costly, you may come to the moment when you will have to fight with all the odds against you and only a precarious chance for survival. There may be a worse case. You may have to fight when there is no hope of victory, because it is better to perish than to live as slaves."[403]

---

[403] Quote DB, accessed 6-23-19
https://www.quotedb.com/quotes/2531

Looking at the increasing speed with which the Progressive regime (read Deep State) is building its command and control structure, the future is invading the present at an ever accelerating pace. Their living document has made the Constitution a dead letter. Their mixed economy has as many people on the dole as on the job. The Fed's printing press is burying us, our children, and their grandchildren taking out a mortgage on lives that haven't been lived and spending money from taxes on work that hasn't been done.

We must unite if these United States are to once again become the land of the free and the home of the brave instead of the land of the free lunch and the home of the knave.

Quoting Ben Franklin, "We must hang together, gentlemen...else, we shall most assuredly hang separately."[404]

Today we have a chance. President Trump is dedicated to draining the swamp. The

---

[404] Brainyquote, accessed 6-23-19
https://www.brainyquote.com/search_results?q=We
+must+hang+together%2C+gentlemen...else%2C+
we+shall+most+assuredly+hang+separately

swamp is equally dedicated to getting rid of Trump. Their embedded judges make rulings which are not even pretending to follow the law to thwart him. The Russian collusion witch hunt continues to provide cover for Hillary's actual crimes by trying to invent ones with which to impeach The Donald.

I will end with one more quote from Winston Churchill, "Never give in, never give in, never, never, never, never—in nothing, great or small, large or petty— never give in except to convictions of honor and good sense."[405]

---

[405] Goalcast, accessed 6-23-19
https://www.goalcast.com/2017/06/20/top-24-winston-churchill-quotes-to-inspire-you-to-never-surrender/

Drain the Swamp

Dispatch Fifty-four

A Coup Wrapped in a Hoax
Inside a Vendetta

After 675 days of investigation, 2,800 subpoenas, 500 warrants, and 500 witness interviews here are a few things that never happened in the time-consuming, money-wasting, slanderous attempt to erase the results of the 2016 election known as the Mueller investigation:

1. After endless speculation and daily smears Donald Trump Jr., Jared Kushner, and other people whose supposed legal jeopardy was the subject of around-the-clock media speculation in the last year were not indicted.

2. No one in the Trump campaign or his inner circle was implicated or charged with conspiring with Russia to fix the 2016 election, as the media authoritatively

417

claimed day-after-day throughout the last two years.

3. The president was not subpoenaed though the almost hysterical pundits of the propaganda arm of the Democrat Party known as the drive-by media assured us he would be.

4. Though endless hours of speculation centered on the President's imminent firing of Mueller it never happened

5. The ceaseless attacks against President Trump disguised as news constantly told us the President obstructed justice by interfering with the Mueller investigation. However, in a letter to Congress, Attorney General Barr after mentioning he was required to notify lawmakers if any top Justice Department officials ever interfered with the Mueller investigation stated, "There were no such instances."

Completing an investigation initiated by the CABAL in the Justice Department dedicated to reversing the outcome of the 2016 election, an investigation which did not meet the Justice Department's own standard for appointing a Special Prosecutor; the presence of an underlying crime, Mueller is finally finished. Not long after the news broke, Fox News White House correspondent John Roberts said, "The feeling at the White House right now is that this is finally over."

Unfortunately for those of us who want to get about the business of making America great again this will probably be a yes and a no. Mueller's report not recommending any additional indictments doesn't mean that the Democrats have given up on their eternal Trump-Russia investigation. Since those who knew there was nothing to this in the first place anticipated this possibility. This is why the House Democrats jump started new Trump-Russia investigations to ensure it will never be over. Does anyone doubt such investigations will continue, at least until the 2020 elections? In reality this has been and is government funded media fueled opposition research and Democrat campaigning for whichever socialist they eventually nominate.

Drain the Swamp

During one of their relentless wall-to-wall bash Trump panels even the dying CNN, nest of the most outspoken of the so-called journalists suffering from Trump Derangement Syndrome, had to admit this was a "Huge Victory for the President," and that Trump was "Vindicated."

Here are few samplings from their less than enthusiastic announcement of their long sought dream: the end of the Mueller investigation.

Their Commander Wolf Blitzer said, "President Trump has won a huge victory."

Evan Pérez commented, "He's been vindicated by them."

The rabidly anti-Trump Gloria Borger agreed, "And then he's now vindicated, exactly." She added, "You know–how do you manage that politically? I mean, we obviously can't jump the gun here. We have to see what comes out from Barr, and what's in the report. But if I'm at Mar-A-Lago with the president, as Pamela has been reporting, the lawyers are ... that I would be very happy."

Another of CNN's trained talking heads Shimon Prokupecz said, "A couple of victories here. The president did not have to sit down for an interview. They were so concerned about that, because he'd get caught up in lies–and there'd be perjury traps. Okay, so that's now over. No more people being indicted. Sealed, unsealed–no more indictments. Mueller is done. Huge victory for the president."

The uncompromising off the rails nature of these investigations is exemplified in their incessant demands for President Trump's tax returns. He's been audited by the IRS every year for more than a dozen years. Does anyone believe if the highly politicized Obama IRS of Commissioner Douglas Shulman and Lois Lerner had found any irregularities in Trump's returns they wouldn't have been leaked? Does anyone in the Democrat echo chamber media ever mention that Nancy Pelosi refuses to make her tax returns public?

So one chapter may be ending but never fear the sequels are here. It is all about damaging President Trump enough so that he will lose his bid for re-election. Add the votes of the low-information and indoctrinated by the nightly news sheep to the illegals, the felons, the socialists, and the America Last crowd and the Democrats hope to deliver us to Bernie, Beto, and their Green New Deal brand of Venezuelan worker's paradise.

Let's hope there're enough people who've swallowed the red pill, had the scales wiped from their eyes, and realize the entire Trump – Russia side show was designed to front for a silent coup and to cover up the only real colluding that took place in the 2016 election. Hillary colluding with DNC to rig the nomination process against Bernie. And Hillary's campaign colluding with Fusion GPS who hired former British spy Christopher Steele to compile a "dossier" filled with fake news and garbage that was all dressed up by the FBI, taken to the FISA Court, and presented as a legitimate intelligence document. Let's hope.

Dispatch Fifty-five

Who Weaponized the FBI?

With the release of the Mueller Report we finally have what should be the definitive word: There never was any collusion between President Trump or his campaign and the Russian government. After 675 days of investigation, 2,800 subpoenas, 500 warrants, and 500 witness interviews nada, zip, nothing but false charges, innuendo, slander, and an obvious smear campaign by the sore losers and their megaphone media.

The beginning of this sordid chapter in American History is almost laughable. After former Attorney General Jeff Sessions recused himself[406] from his job Deputy Attorney General Rod J. Rosenstein sends a letter to President Trump recommending he

---

[406] Bernson, T., *Time*, 3-2-17, accessed 6-23-19 https://time.com/4689492/jeff-sessions-russia-recuse/

fire DBI director James Comey for his handling of the investigation into former Secretary of State Hillary Clinton's private email server.[407] Then Rosenstein appoints a Special Counsel to investigate supposed collusion between the Trump campaign and Vladimir Putin because President Trump fired Comey in an attempt to obstruct of justice. You just can't make this stuff up.

With the release of Mueller's report the first act in the silent coup has collapsed.

Now comes the time to pay the piper. There are increasing cries to investigate the investigators. It's high time the American people find out who weaponized the FBI and then used them in an illegal attempt to influence an election and once that failed to overthrow a duly elected president.

Rep. Devin Nunes (R. CA) the top Republican on the House Intelligence Committee plans to send eight criminal referrals to the Department of Justice.

---

[407] Norwoood, C. & Elaine Godfrey, *The Atlantic*, 5-10-17, accessed 6-23-19 https://www.theatlantic.com/politics/archive/2017/05/rosenstein-letter-annotated/526116/

Calling the gang-that-couldn't-shoot-straight "Watergate Wannabees" Nunes said the criminal activity includes leaks of highly classified material and conspiracies to lie to Congress and the Foreign Intelligence Surveillance Act (FISA) court.[408]

Nunes went on to say that five of the referrals "are what I would call straight up referrals... that name someone and name the specific crimes... [which are] lying to Congress, misleading Congress, leaking classified information."[409]

He also added that "There are three [referrals] that I think are more complicated... We believe there was a conspiracy to lie to the FISA court, mislead the FISA court by numerous individuals that all need to be investigated and looked at that, and we believe the [relevant] statute is the conspiracy statute. The second conspiracy one is involving manipulation of

---

[408] Freeman, B., *Newsmax*, 4-7-19, accessed 6-23-19 https://www.newsmax.com/newsfront/devin-nunes-referrals-russia-probe/2019/04/07/id/910578/
[409] Ibid.

intelligence that also could ensnarl many Americans."[410]

This is not just a Republican witch hunt in response to the Democrat witch hunt.

Ex-Gov. / Sen. Bob Kerrey (D. NE) says, "Rather than investigating the president further, Congress needs to investigate how the Department of Justice got this one so wrong. If the president of the United States is vulnerable to prosecutorial abuse, then God help all the rest of us."[411]

Former Harvard Professor and legal expert Alan Dershowitz, a self-declared liberal Democrat, has maintained from the start that Congress needs a nonpartisan commission to investigate the failings of the justice system in searching for a crime that was not found in the Mueller Report.[412]

The collapse of the Mueller investigation hasn't stopped those who suffer from Trump

---

[410] Ibid.
[411] Mack, E., *Newsmax*, 4-7-19, accessed 6-23-19 https://www.newsmax.com/politics/democrats-bobkerrey-fbi-justicedepartment/2019/04/07/id/910559/
[412] Ibid.

Derangement Syndrome who infest Congress. The current smear being perpetrated by the never-say-die Watergate Wannabees and their silent coup is obstruction of Justice. Since collusion is not a crime and there never was any collusion to begin with how could there have been any obstruction of justice? If anything it should be obstruction of injustice.

Lying to Congress, leaking classified material, lying to obtain FISA warrants, conspiracy to influence a presidential election, and conspiracy to overthrow the president of the United States: this sounds like a plot from the TV series 24. All we need is the dramatic music to make it a real nail biter. If Rep. Nunes starts whispering like Jack Bauer I'm going to move to the edge of my seat.

Conclusion

The Times They Are a Changing

I now have college students who not only look at the Cold War the way my generation looked at WW II, they see Vietnam the way we saw WWI, and they weren't alive on 9-11-01.

They've been force fed on Al Gore's man-made global warming hoax and the glories of the eternally free as outlined by Bernie-style Socialism every day of their legally mandated attendance at public screwals. They don't just say they're Socialists they're proud to tell you they're Socialists. When you ask them what Socialism is after they say, "Everybody gets everything for free," a blank stare usually spreads across their self-satisfied face.

If you point out that Socialism has never worked anywhere ever they point to Bernie,

Drain the Swamp

AOC, and other prominent Democrat fellow-travelers and repeat the mantra about Norway, Sweden, and the Scandinavian Socialist mirage. Their eyes glaze over and they react like Will Robinson's robot when something doesn't compute if you try to tell them that all of the Scandinavian countries have economies that're more capitalistic than our own. Or, that spending less than one percent of GDP on defense because we defend them frees up money for social spending.

A few years ago they were repeating the words of Sean Penn and other Hollywood know-nothings who praised the so-called Socialist miracle in Venezuela. Now that the once fourth richest country in the world has descended into the Socialist end game of living in the dirt and eating leaves the Socialist apologists say its America's fault the miracle has vanished instead of facing the reality that sooner or later you always run out of other people's money.

Hopefully once these preprogrammed proto-adults mature they'll live out the reality of one of the nuggets of wisdom often

attributed to Winston Churchill, "If you're
not a liberal when you're 25, you have no
heart. If you're not a conservative by the
time you're 35, you have no brain."

It's easy to think everything should be free
when your parents have supplied you with
everything for free all your life. Once you
have to figure out how to keep a roof over
your head and food on the table most
people are smart enough to realize there is
in fact no free lunch.

The unfortunate reality is that all of these
dreamy-eyed Kum ba yah kadets may well
vote us all into the Gulag before the reality
of a work-a-day world has a chance to
wring the "I want what I want and I want it
now!" childishness out of their minds.

There's no doubt that the future belongs to
the young for they'll be living in it after the
old are gone. It's also true that very
generation when they're young act as if
youth is some kind of novel invention
they've devised on their own. Today we're
witnessing the abandonment and rejection
of everything that made this country great,
its culture, its history, and its heritage.

Drain the Swamp

Whether America will still be a shining city on a hill and the last best hope of humanity for freedom once the foundations have been swept away is a question for the future to answer. However, one thing is for sure; the times they are a changing.

Enjoy these other books by Dr. Owens

Political Commentary:

The Constitution Failed

Constitutional Philosophy in Action

Then Came Trump

History:

America Won the Vietnam War

The Azusa Street Revival

The More Things Change The More They
Stay The Same

America: Vol 1 Colonial American History

COGIC History: The Dark Years

Religion:

Faith

Novels:

1.   America's Trojan War (Series

2.   America's Odyssey: You Can't Go Home Again

3.   America's Odyssey II: You Must Go Home Again

4.   America's Steel Horse Brigade

5.   America's Armageddon

All these titles are available from Amazon in paperback and Kindle

www.ingramcontent.com/pod-product-compliance
Lightning Source LLC
Chambersburg PA
CBHW060446290526
45791CB00001B/2